C000242892

BEYOND THE HIMALAYAS

M. MacDONALD-BAYNE

M.C., PH.D., D.D.

(Principal: College of Universal Science)

Author of: *The Higher Power You Can Use, I am the Life, Heal Yourself, Spiritual and Mental Healing, What is Mine is Thine (Parts I and II), How to Relax and Revitalise Yourself, Divine Healing of Mind and Body (The Master Speaks Again), Your Life Renewed Every Day (The Greatest Tonic in the World)*

Published by Audio Enlightenment Press.Com

Giving Voice to the Wisdom of the Ages

Copyright © 2014 by Audio Enlightenment Press

All rights reserved. No part of this publication may be reproduced, distributed, or transmitted in any form or by any means, including photocopying, recording, or other electronic or mechanical methods, without the prior written permission of the publisher, except in the case of brief quotations embodied in critical reviews and certain other noncommercial uses permitted by copyright law.

Printed in the United States of America

First Printing, 2014

1 2 3 4 5 6 7 8 9 10

ISBN 978-1-941489-13-0

www.AudioEnlightenmentPress.Com

A GNOSTIC AUDIO SELECTION

First AudioEnlightenmentPress.Com Printing

April 2014

Editor's Foreword

Dr. Murdo MacDonald-Bayne was born in Scotland in 1887. During his lifetime he traveled throughout the world healing thousands of people of all kinds of diseases, and teaching the Truth of the Law of Being to many thousands more. Murdo MacDonald-Bayne was fondly referred to as Dr.Mac by his students, who often spoke of seeing him overshadowed by a higher being during his lectures. It is said that he journeyed several times into India and Tibet where he spent long periods (recounted in *Beyond the Himalayas* and its sequel, *The Yoga of the Christ*) in the company of true Masters of the Tibetan Himalayas.

He often spoke about his books and teachings being undiscovered for a period of time and then entering a new era of resurgence. I believe now is the time for people to discover, or rediscover, the works of this great man.

This edition is based on the original manuscripts and we have kept the original spellings of words (i.e. criticise instead of criticize, organisations instead of organizations) to keep the integrity of the original manuscript. It is our purpose to maintain and present lost spiritual classics, not to edit them to meet our needs.

This is also a Gnostic Audio Selection, which means that in addition to an incredible read, you have access to the streaming audio book version, for those days when you just want to kick back and enjoy a great audio book. Information for accessing the streaming audio is in the resource section at the back of the book.

We are republishing *Beyond the Himalayas* (as well as *The Yoga of the Christ*) by Dr.Bayne, and more titles when they become available. If you are a student of spirituality and metaphysics you owe it to yourself to read the works of this incredible healer and teacher.

Barry J. Peterson

TABLE OF CONTENTS

FOREWORD   Page i

INTRODUCTION   Page v

CHAPTER I   Page 1

CHAPTER II   Page 19

CHAPTER III   Page 39

CHAPTER IV   Page 61

CHAPTER V   Page 79

CHAPTER VI   Page 95

CHAPTER VII   Page 117

CHAPTER VIII   Page 137

CHAPTER IX   Page 127

CHAPTER X   Page 183

CHAPTER XI   Page 207

CHAPTER XII   Page 223

RESOURCES   Page 241

FOREWORD

To you, the reader of this book, I want to say, this book is not written merely as a history of my travels in Tibet, neither is it meant to be a display of words to reveal the Truth, for the Truth cannot be revealed in words. Neither should it be read from an intellectual point of view so as to give pleasure to the mind; nor is it meant to give you a new religion or a new authority or belief.

It is meant to open up, to awaken the inner Being that is closed up, asleep, to become aware of the powers and possibilities of the Real Self, so that you are no longer the little personality with a limited life, but a centre of Universal action and in direct contact with Cosmic Forces. Then you will no longer be the unwilling plaything of fate but a conscious Master of Nature, liberated from the imprisoned smallness and sufferings of the gross human body.

It will take you beyond every mental idealistic culture of ideas and ideals belonging to the mind, which are only half-truths.

It shows you how to bring the supramental power of the Divine Conciousness into the ignorant mind, transforming the mind and body, thereby creating a Divine Life in matter.

To the critic I would say, do not criticise anything you know nothing about. If your beliefs prevent you from accepting what I say, you will know why by reading this book with an open mind.

To the dogmatist, this book can only help you when you understand what dogma is and how you have acquired it.

To the reviewer, do no review this book if you do not understand yourself - otherwise it will expose your lack of wisdom.

To the earnest seeker, I do not want you to accept what I say or it may become another belief.

Foreword

A belief only hinders the revealing of the Truth. Believing or disbelieving, accepting or rejecting, will not give you understanding. Cleanse your mind first by discerning impersonally all you have read or heard, and you will find a silence that is not of time in which the Truth will be revealed to you.

To the atheist, you think you are a disbeliever but you have just another belief which prevents you from understanding. Search your mind and see what formulations you have created there; then you will realise how ignorant you are of the Real Truth.

To those who are caught up in the various philosophies, religious organisations, etc., I would say, examine what these are first before you read this book or you will be merely reading you own conditioning into it. Free your mind from all fear, superstition and belief, and then there will be an immediate transformation, for the Truth is Eternal and Ever-present in the Now.

Immediately you get rid of your mental formulations, your imitations, by understanding what they are and how they have come about, the Truth will be revealed instantly. Truth is not a matter of time or becoming.

Becoming is always to-morrow---this is going away from Reality-Truth. Being now, is Truth. If Truth is not Now, it will never be to-morrow. Living in the Now, moment to moment, this is Truth.

There cannot be any memory, or right or wrong, past or future, when you live in the Now; there can only be Love and Affection which *is* Truth.

Being Now, is Real; Being Now, is loving and truly living: Being Now, is Eternal Life in which there is no death. All else is made up in your mind.

Your reactions will tell you how your mind is made up, because Truth is not made up, and has no reaction. It is the mind that reacts according to its conditioning; therefore watch your reactions and you will see how you are caught up.

Everyone reacts differently according to his or her mental make-up.

If you believe or if you disbelieve, if you reject or accept, if you feel that it is disturbing your pet ideas, your religious beliefs, if you are in any way mentally disturbed, it shows that you are not free. Your reactions may be automatic, which shows you are bound, hand and foot.

Note your reactions and you will understand the self with its bundle of theories, its formulations, its likes and dislikes, beliefs, ideas, its hates, its jealousies, its antagonisms, its wants. Then you will know how far you are from the Truth.

Geshi Rimpoche, who is mentioned in this book, has passed from the physical and I have since spoken to him, proving that there is no separation except in the mind of man.

My friend is still in the flesh in Tibet, and though he has travelled in the astral many times since helping me in my work, his name is purposely not mentioned, at his own request, so that he may not be troubled by curiosity-seekers in and out of Asia.

THE AUTHOR

INTRODUCTION

In my introduction to my book *The Higher Power You Can Use* I wrote the following words:

"I feel it is a great honour to be the bearer of this message to the world; but I do not claim any special privilege, nor do I claim any spiritual quality that makes me any different from my fellow-men.

"For many years I have been an earnest worker and a student of the Inner Teachings, healing the sick and teaching what I knew of the Truth all over the world, and I have met with a very large measure of success. For this I alone was not wholly responsible - as I now know -having been spiritually helped and guided throughout all these years of probation.

"It was not until one night when a mysterious Visitor appeared to me that I knew what my real mission was. He spoke these words: 'I have been with you a long time but you knew it not. But now the time has come for me to make myself known to you. I will guide you to the Himalayas in Tibet, where you shall receive instructions for your real mission. Many are called but few are chosen; are you prepared to leave all and follow me? Fear not, for the world will rejoice - the message you will bear will take away the confusion from the minds of the people; and those who will hear you are my people. I will be by your side and your strength shall not fail, for whom God has chosen He shall sustain.' Then he took his departure as silently as he had come.

"From that time on I was directed step by step to the great Himalayas in Tibet; and there in the hidden recesses of the majestic snow-clad mountains where the atmosphere is so clear and the vibrations so pure that heaven opens on to the earth, in that glorious state where heaven and earth are as one, I was instructed what to do and where to go. During my sojourn there I witnessed spiritual manifestations so wonderful that words utterly fail to describe them.

Later I will present to the world, in book form details of these happenings---what I saw and heard, also my travels and experiences, with descriptions of the way to the most inaccessible parts of the Great Tibetan Himalayas. I shall also reveal the joys and ecstasy of meeting daily with the Masters, whose love, sympathy and simplicity is the secret of their mighty Power. For Love is God and God is Love. 'For He so loved the world that He sent His only begotten Son, that they who hearken unto Him will find eternal immortality.' When the Soul is ready the Master appears, and those who are ready will hear and know the Master's voice proclaiming all nations one nation, all peoples one people, all life one Life; one Tree with many branches, but the same Life in all: One in all and all in One.

"I, myself, make no claim; I am just a voice in the wilderness calling to the sons and daughters of God to hearken unto the Truth. For this I was told I was born."

I have since written nine other books, the names of which appear on the front page.

Now the time has come to write the book I promised in my introduction to *The Higher Power You Can Use.*

Firstly, I am going to tell you something about myself and how the desire for this great adventure first came into my life.

This is by no means an autobiography, for I would not like to write my own, I will leave that for someone else.

Many people have asked me why I went to Tibet. Well, behind it all there is a fascinating story and I will make it as clear and brief as possible.

In most people's lives there is a living force that is seldom realised, pushing them on to a goal of which they had no idea. That was the case in my life.

Introduction

Now this book is neither a literary display of words nor a fairy tale; neither is it a book to reveal the Truth - no book can ever do that. I will write jut as the thoughts and occurrences come into my mind.

If you read this book aloud it will benefit you even more; for the Spirit alone has voice.

CHAPTER I

I was born and brought up in the Highlands of Scotland. As a boy I remember well the many psychic experiences which began for me at the early age of seven years.

The invisible world, from which only a veil separates us, was as clear to me as the physical, for I was born with this gift, if one could call it a gift, and I am sure that all have it, though they know it not.

I would relate some of these experiences to my parents, and what I knew, but they did no encourage me --- I was too accurate for most people's liking!

When I was quite young and going to school, some books came into my possession, yet I do not know how. They were books of the ancient Yoga and you may think it strange, but I seemed to know and understand with a clarity that amazed my elders.

Yet there was something these books could not tell me. I could not explain what it was.

But now, when I look back, I must have known what it was. The fact was, these books gave me only an idea, but an idea is not the thing itself, and I have since realised this fully.

The word "Life" or the idea of Life is not Life; neither is the word "God" God. Every preacher and teacher is trying to tell you what Life is, yet they can give you only an idea of It, and that is not Life. It is because we have so many different ideas that we have so much separation and strife in religion, groups and nationalities in the world today.

I was about seven years old when I saw the face of the Master Jesus. It was a living face animated with Life, not the reflection of a picture that my senses could have seen from a book or reproduction. It was alive and living just like you and me.

1

Chapter I

The effect on me was too much, and I was put to bed and lived on rum and milk with a beaten-up egg in it. This was my only food. The doctor said my heart had moved two inches out of its place.

This bed business was boring me to tears, when one morning I heard a voice saying, "Get up! Go outside, run and jump!" I did so and was well from that moment. This convinced me more than ever that there was no death, that others besides those in the physical were alive, and I was determined to find out more about it. What amazed the doctors was that I was one hundred per cent fit from that very moment.

It was after this that I found that I could jump from a great height and hold myself almost in mid-air and come down lightly on my toes. Although I could not yet understand the meaning of it all, I had read about it in the Yoga books which were my treasured possessions.

I read how the Yogi could levitate themselves, and I must have been doing something similar without a knowledge of the methods used.

The many things I did fearlessly caused my parents very many anxious moments.

Although they knew I was different from the others, yet their anxiety about me still remained and I was very conscious of this fact.

The winter nights were a great pleasure to me. I used to sit in front of the huge log fire in our ancestral home, my right foot always on the railing in front of the fire and my jacket on the back of my chair. In my boyhood days, I always wore Scotland's national dress, the comfortable kilt, up to the age of fifteen years, and often wore it at the Highland games in which I took part whenever the opportunity arose.

Above the mantelpiece hung the great claymore that my forefathers had fought with in many battles, including the battle of Culloden Moor.

On both sides of the mantelpiece were swords and pistols that the Clan MacDonald had used in their raids on the Lowlands and over the English border.

I would listen intently to my father telling us of the many stories of adventure of the MacDonald clan, he would also relate some of his own adventures, for he had visited many foreign lands and we used to listen to these stories over and over again. I never tired of them and they fostered in me that wanderlust, coupled with my mind's desire for knowledge, that was to lead me away into so many parts of the world. As I grew older this passion grew stronger and stronger. I began to spread my wings to take flight to distant lands.

All Scotch people are adamant that their children should have a good education, so I was sent to the university and though I studied medicine it had no appeal for me; it was like treating some dead thing, when I knew that Life was the only living power. Yet this background helped me later in my work of healing all over the world. Some of the miraculous results I will explain later in another book.

I made up my mind to go to India, and there I found the Yogi and gained a great deal of wisdom and knowledge, but I was not yet satisfied, even though it was leading me to the goal I desired. Although I had visited India several times I was still not satisfied.

I sailed up the Persian Gulf to Basra. From there I trekked up the Tigris River and crossed over the desert to the Euphrates. I lived

3

with the Arabs and roamed the ancient city of Baghdad with all its picturesque mosques and minarets, explored the ancient ruins of Babylon,and searched ancient Persia and Palestine for relics of old Bible stories.

When the first World War came in 1914 I joined a Highland Regiment, became a commissioned officer and was awarded the Military Cross, also a foreign decoration for saving life under gun-fire and was wounded four times in doing so. After the war I again went to India, through China and Japan. I went to French Indo-China where I explored the ancient Cambodian ruins of a civilisation that seemed to have disappeared overnight and left behind magnificent relics as the only evidence of its existence.

I then crossed Canada from east to west and west to east, motored more than six thousand miles in the United States and visited Mexico and South America. I trekked through Africa and explored the ancient ruins of Zimbabwe in Rhodesia where, it is said, a civilization existed four thousand years ago, and around which Rider Haggard wrote his books *She* and *King Solomon's Mines*. Similar ruins have been found in Brazil and I think that the similarity of the ruins point to something in common. Some day our achaeologists may throw some light on the origin of this ancient civilisation.

I retraced the steps of Livingstone and Stanley and explored the Zambesi River above the mighty Victoria Falls. I studied the ruins of ancient Egypt and visited most places in Europe, also travelled through Australia and New Zealand and the South Pacific Islands. I travelled to the four corners of the earth and sailed the seven seas. I did healing and teaching all over the world and became well-known on the four continents, but the greatest adventure of my life had not yet been fulfilled---my journey into the forbidden land of mysterious Tibet, the roof of the world.

Chapter I

I had a unique experience. Already I had given up hope of ever reaching my goal and then a figure appeared to me telling me to go to Africa, from where I would again go to India.

The figure gave me all details of the route I should take, telling me that I would be met by someone who would guide me in person beyond the Himalayas.

(This interesting and extraordinary incident comes back to mind, and I must relate it because it has a bearing on what followed. I had just come away from Tibet and was giving my first lecture in Montreal, Canada. It happened like this. I had been lecturing for about half-anhour, everyone was seated, and the doors were closed. Mrs. Chisholm and the ushers were standing in the foyer outside, when the figure of a man appeared as from nowhere and said:

"Tell him I am pleased he has done what I asked of him." No sooner than the words were said the figure disappeared. This was seen by several people. I knew the answer, but they did not.

Some are still talking about this experience; only the other day I had a letter from a lady in Montreal who was there when the incident took place and she referred to it in her letter.)

You can well imagine the excitement that set my heart beating as the ship *Inchanga* sailed up the Hoogli River into Calcutta (this ship I had boarded at Durban, South Africa).

The great moment was near, and though this was the fifth time I had been to India there was something new and fresh about it. To meet someone I had never seen in the flesh was a thrilling anticipation.

As the ship drew into the wharf the babbling voices of hundreds of coolies drowned my conversation with the people around me.

Chapter I

I lost no time in getting ashore, and I was soon surrounded by dozens of willing hands mostly looking for rupees and annas. But having been to India several times I had learned their ways and was able to speak in a language they understood.

I searched all round, looking for someone to recognise me, and as no one appeared I was crestfallen. Was all this a hoax, I wondered? After most of the passengers had left I got my own luggage on its way and proceeded to the Grand Hotel situated in the Chowringee, opposite the Calcutta Domain.

I settled there for a few days and visited my old friends Swami Yogananda and Swami Ramana, also a few more of the Yogi I knew. I discussed my problems with them and they advised me not to give up but to go on over the Himalayas and beyond if necessary, and I was sure to meet the one who spoke to me.

So in the afternoon I took a taxi to the railway station to arrange my train transport to Siliguri in northern Bengal, the furthest point to which the main railway goes towards the Great Himalayas.

The taxi-driver, a Sikh with an angelic face, regarded me as a raw tourist and was taking me for a ride, for he proceeded in the opposite direction. I knew his game and decided to teach him a lesson. So when we finally reached the station he said, "Five rupees, Sahib!" I handed him two rupees, which was more than the normal fare, and I told him in his own language that he was lucky I did not report him for his was a serious offence. You should have seen his face! The angelic look disappeared, and without a murmur, disgusted with himself, he drove off.

In the evening I visited a Colonel friend of mine who was with me when I was attached to the Indian Army. He was a student of the deeper things of Life and we had enjoyed a close friendship till he passed from this earth into the higher Life. Since he passed he has no doubt satisfied his deep desire for greater wisdom and knowledge.

He put on mufti (civilian clothes) and we went down to the Bhodi Institute, a select Indian club, where the Hindu professors, doctors, Yogi and the like congregated.

My friend, Professor Shastra, a professor in the Calcutta University, was giving an address on Ancient Sanskrit, on which he was considered the greatest authority in the world.

Ancient Sanskrit is the writing of an Ancient Indian culture seemingly far in advance of any of our culture in the West, even today.

It was not long before I was recognised and after the address I was immediately invited to the platform and was asked to give an account of my wanderings since I was last in their midst and what I was doing now. So I told them, and I must say that their interest was profound.

Some of the great Indian teachers were there, including Sri Aurobindo (of whom I wrote in my book *Spiritual and Mental Healing*), Swami Yogananda, Swami Ramana the great Indian scientist, Tagore India's national poet, and the great Gandhi himself, besides many more of India's leading lights.

My Colonel friend turned to me and said, "I abhor the inflated idea of superiority of some of our own people here in India which prevents them from understanding the higher things of Life, and when they leave they are even more inflated, but only with their own ignorance unfortunately, which goes to show the depraved state of their immature mentality. In the world it is the humble that are great, and we only become humble when we begin to get wisdom, and when we acquire wisdom we are humbler still. This germ of greatness must be born in the forthcoming generation or we are doomed to complete oblivion." I agreed with him and so do all right-thinking people.

Two days later I took my departure from Calcutta in the train bound for Siliguri. You have to keep your carriage doors locked on the inside, otherwise your compartment will be overrun with all kinds of people, notwithstanding the fact that you have your compartment reserved, and a notice to that effect displayed on the outside. This, however, makes no difference to the travelling mob, and it is a most difficult job to get them out once they get in.

When I reached Siliguri, the end of the main railway to northern Bengal, I saw the little mountain railway train that would take me further on towards the Himalayas. As I changed from one train to the other I sensed a nasty smell, and on looking round I saw a leper holding out what were at one time hands, now covered in dirty sacking. Lepers were not allowed to come nearer than within three feet of you.

I took pity on the leper and handed him a rupee, when an Indian policeman came along and hit him with his cane. I remonstrated him and said, "You are hitting yourself, do you know that?"

With an amazed look on his face, I left him wondering, and walked of, letting him think it out for himself.

Lepers today are mostly allowed their freedom; previously they were hounded down and placed in leper colonies. This sent many into hiding and they spread the disease. But now they are treated with injections of combination of chalmurga oil and other new drugs which have been very successful in the termination of the disease.

The little mountain railway carriages were only up to my shoulder; the tiny engine was painted green, and all the carriages were painted red. I had to bend down to enter in, and while sitting, my head touched the roof. One could hardly credit that such a tiny engine had power enough to draw about a dozen carriages behind it up very steep grades. My thoughts turned to the steam that made it possible. This thought made me realise that it is the Life that makes it possible for us to do all the things we do; the body has no power of its own, just as the engine has no power of its own.

Thus I started off on a further stage of my journey. We crawled under viaducts making complete circles, looping the loop, crossing over the very viaduct that we crawled under about half-an-hour before, and still we crawled higher and higher up the mountainside. Zig-zagging and looping the loop, we proceeded on our way till we reached about five thousand feet, where we stopped at a place called Gillikola, and here I got off.

The train goes as far as Darjeeling, which is the main town in Nepal, and it is situated at the foot of the great Himalayas.

On the platform were waiting a number of sturdy little mountain women not more than four feet in height, each with a strap over her head, hanging over her shoulders and down her back. They immediately came forward and put the hanging strap under the heavy boxes and lifted them as if they were so many matchboxes.

I was amazed to see their strength, but I found it was a knack; the drag was across the forehead and over the shoulders, the weight resting on the back. I was told that one of these women carried a piano all the way from Kalimpong to Darjeeling, a matter of thirty-odd miles.

I took the car I had ordered to meet me at Gillikola, and off we went, still climbing and zig-zagging up the mountain till we reached Kalimpong. This town in the Himalayas is the starting point of the trade route between India, Sikkim and Tibet. From here everything

Chapter I

is taken over road and tracks which become very narrow, in some parts not more than a few feet wide.

In Kalimpong I found a motley crowd of people, Indians, Tibetans, people from Sikkim, people from Nepal, people from Bhutan, and quite a number of White people who were taking their holidays in the mountain air, away from the heat and the humidity of Calcutta.

The hill states of Nepal, Sikkim and Bhutan separate India from Tibet. So Kalimpong becomes even a more important town than Darjeeling, especially as the trade route starts there.

Here I gathered together my caravan, which included an interpreter, a personal bearer and bodyguard, a man who knew the ropes of all the brigands roaming the trade routes. I hired a Tibetan pony for myself, one for my interpreter, one for my bodyguard, and one for my Indian bearer, two mules as pack-animals and three porters.

All goods coming from and going to Tibet are carried on the backs of donkeys, mules and porters. From Kalimpong they are transported by road and rail to Calcutta, thence to other destinations. The tea that comes from Darjeeling is conveyed by the mountain railway to Siliguri, the on the main railway to Calcutta, then shipped to all parts of the world.

In Kalimpong I met a namesake, a Mr. MacDonald who kept the Himalayan Hotel. He was half-Tibetan, the son of a Mr. MacDonald from Scotland, at one time British trade agent at Yatung in Tibet, and who had married a Tibetan woman.

Mr. Macdonald and I became friends. He could speak Tibetan, Hindustani and English perfectly, and I got down to learning as

Chapter I

much of Tibetan as I could in the time I was with him. I could already speak Hindustani and this helped quite a lot.

I had to wait in Kalimpong until my permit to enter Tibet arrived, and during this period I gave much thought to the stranger whom I was to meet. I anticipated that I would have to go as far as Tibet to find him. He had met me neither in Calcutta nor in Kalimpong when I arrived, but I considered it would be foolish to turn back. I must go on. Something inside me said, "You must go on."

I had been there for three days when I was walking down towards the town from the house I was staying in. I saw a man dressed in a purple gown slightly more purple than the Lama cloak. I could not take my eyes off him, so much did he attract me.

He came straight up to me and said, "You have arrived, my son," in perfect English. I was so taken aback that I could not speak at once, for I had no thought of being met at Kalimpong now, especially as I had not been met on my arrival.

He put his right hand on my left shoulder and I felt as if I was charged with electricity.

Then he said, "I have been with you a long time, but you knew it not." I knew those words, they had rung in my mind for a very long time.

Then he revealed what he knew about me, the things I did and the things I should have done, and perhaps the things I should not have done, which after all, he explained, did not matter very much.

I knew that he must have been with me for a very long time because my life to him was an open book, and there was no use telling him where I had been. What I wanted most now was to try to let him know what I knew. So I began to discourse on philosophy and higher metaphysics. I went on for some time (I could not tell you how long, for time seemed to disappear) and he listened to me very quietly. I thought that I had made an impression, at least I would be worthy of his interest in me. Then he uttered these words:

"My son, it does not matter very much whether it is true or not, does it?" If you had struck me with a sledgehammer I could not have been more stunned. Then I heard him say to me:

"I will see you tomorrow, my son, and all is being arranged for your journey.

Everything is being taken care of."

He then turned and went down the path, leaving me totally empty---that is what I was, empty!

I thought deeply about what he had said, in those few words, and it completely changed me. I could see that all I had, was made up in my mind. I had missed the greatest thing in my life --- the Living Present.

What I had, were mere words, ideas, images. What a fool I had been all these years.

And how thankful I was for those few words! I knew that at last I would find that for which I was seeking.

The following day he came early, with a smile of satisfaction, and said: "My son, I see that you have had your first lesson of the Truth that sets men free. You were bound, but now I see that you have begun to free yourself."

"But," I said, "you did it!"

Chapter I

"Oh no," he said, "my words could not have done it unless you were ready to receive."

Then he said: "You will leave here a week today when your pass will arrive. I want you to go through the jungle, along by the Teesta River and up through Sikkim to Gangtok; I want you to have the experience of the jungle as well. From Gangtok you will cross the Natula Pass on into Yatung, the first town in Tibet. You will then have further instructions from me."

That week in Kalimpong was one of great joy, a joy of anticipation. Only once did I see him before I left and I was determined to ask him one question.

I said to him, "Meditation to be has been a difficult problem and I have found it so with others. Could you suggest any way I should meditate?"

He said, "To know how to meditate is a very complex problem. To follow any system, whether it be East or West, is not meditation. If you follow a system you shape your mind according to a particular pattern and this is what you want to avoid."

I said: "I know there is a lot of nonsense taught about meditation by those who know little or nothing about it."

"Yes, my son," he said, "that is true, only too true, and you are one of them who tried to teach this nonsense."

I was not hurt by his remark, because I knew how true it was.

Then he said, "If you condition your mind you cannot be free; meditation must lead to freedom, for only the mind that is free can discover the truth. When you understand the process of your mind, which you will do as we proceed during these months ahead, you will find greater freedom"

Chapter I

(Months ahead! I had no idea of months ahead! But as a fact it was months before I came away, and I could have stayed beyond the Himalayas many more months.)

While I was thinking he seemed to stop and listen to my inaudible thoughts, I at once realised that he knew them.

He smiled and then said, "There can be no freedom through the discipline of any system, for this would only make you more bound than you were before. Real meditation is to discover what is beyond the mind. A particular system prevents the mind from understanding, for it is merely self-hypnosis which is binding and destroying."

Then he stopped while I began to rearrange my thoughts. I was the first to speak again, I said:

"Now I begin to see daylight:

"Yes," he went on, "in freedom alone is there true creativeness, and the mind must be clear of all beliefs, systems, and discipline, free of all conditioning of any kind. Then you can create through your own creativeness and not through the belief or idea of another, which only makes you an imitator. To be aware of the whole process of thinking, you will begin to know yourself and it is this which leads to freedom. If you merely have a belief or an idea then you can never know what is beyond it, but if you know what is a belief, what is an idea, then you can get beyond, and there you will find that which is Real, which is not an idea or a belief, but a Livingness that is Eternal and Everpresent."

Yes, my mind was clearing. I was getting rid of my ideas, my beliefs, my philosophies.

Chapter I

A cleansing was taking place and I knew it. How could I show my gratitude, that was my thought at that moment, when he uttered the words:

"Gratitude is the belief in separation, between yourself and Reality, but there is no separation. It is but the illusion of the mind that is caught up in separation, in beliefs, in ideas and the like."

Then he said, "I have seen you sitting in a corner meditating, trying to focus your mind on an image or an idea to the exclusion of all else, but you were never successful in doing so.

Is it not that other thoughts rose up in your mind to cause a conflict? There can never be a quiet in the midst of conflict! The conflict must cease before there is quiet. Quiet never comes out of conflict. It is only when you understand conflict, that conflict ceases. Quiet is the natural state of the mind that is not in conflict!

"Is it not so," he went on, "that you spent much of your time and energy in this wasteful battle of conflict and gained nothing in the end? You produced mental pictures, but that was an illusion, not the meditation that leads to freedom and the discovery of that which is beyond the mind, which alone is creative."

"Oh!" I thought; I drew a long breath, I felt the freedom I was looking for and his words rang in my mind, "It does not matter very much whether it is true or not." I was trying to make an idea the Truth, to make Reality out of an idea, and it could not be done.

Then he said, "Reality is not made up in the mind. Reality is. You do not make it. It comes into Being when your mind is freed and not before. Then you will know that you are the Truth, that you are Life itself."

I now understood more than I had ever understood all the years of my life. I felt the joy of living in freedom. I could not put it into words---there was something Real that I could not define, but I knew that I was alive, that what I made up in my mind was not Reality.

The Creativeness was within and now I could let it express Itself, and the more free I was from beliefs, from systems, from ideas, the greater It would become. I could see this now!

This was the joy, and I could not hold back. He saw it, for he said in his lovely voice:

"Son, that is all there is."

"Yes," I said; "my meditation was merely a form of self-isolation in which I carried my private memories, my private experiences which were not understood. I know now that my mind could never be free from that conditioning until I understood it."

"Yes," he said, "may I put it this way, you were forcing your mind into a state of self-hypnosis by the constant repetition of words. But the mind that is forced into that state is dead.

Real meditation is a true expression of Life. You only dulled your mind, and when the state ended your conditioning was more apparent, was it not?"

I knew this to be true. Why could I not have seen this before? I thought. Again I knew he was reading my very thoughts.

"Yes," he continued, "you must know the ways of the self, your thoughts, by being impersonally aware of them, looking at yourself in your realisation to others and the things you talk about, just as you would observe someone else. There, in that state, is the echoing of your conditioning which can be observed without condemning, without fear, freed from such conditioning. In this way you will discover yourself, you will see how you have conditioned yourself, through your fear, your condemning, your criticism, your resistance, for these are the ways of the self.

"In this freedom there is neither conflict nor illusion. In this process there is true meditation." Then I said, "I see that freedom which is Truth does not come into being through the search for It but through understanding the whole structure of the self, with all its desires, its prejudices, its conditioning, its cherished illusions, and when these are discerned and understood they dissolve away and what is left is Reality---the Real self."

"Yes, that is true," he answered. "Meditation is the discovery of the Real Self, not separated from other selves, but that which is Whole and complete, which is without conditioning of any kind. That experience is true meditation.

"When you see that your conditioned thought has a beginning and ending in the self, being the product of the mind in bondage, there is silence, not the silence that is willed or the result of hypnotisation but a silence that is not of time, a silence that is not created, but the silence in which the Eternal is revealed, this Silence being Eternity Itself.

"In this Silence there is the state of creation. This is the silence the Master knows and which you also will know. It is the Timeless that is Real, and is not conditioned by memories or experience and where conflict does not exist.

"So without understanding how you have conditioned yourself and merely forced your mind to meditate is a waste of time and energy which only creates more illusion. To know your thoughts and how they arise, and to understand your bondage, is the beginning of wisdom. If you do not understand yourself, meditation has no meaning, for, whatever you project, it is in accordance with your own conditioning and that is obviously not Reality."

Chapter I

I was aware now, aware of the mightiness of Reality. I was aware of the mighty power he possessed and in that humility I knew that God could express himself wholly. His presence conveyed to me that same feeling, but I could not describe it.

He rose up and blessed me. He felt my love go out towards him, for he said, "No one cometh unto me except through the Love of God."

After he had gone I was speechless. It was as though some great mighty Power had come, and left with me a sense of It and I knew it would grow as I got more freedom.

I saw him again in the morning before I began my journey over the Himalayas, and he told me that he would meet me in Yatung. He specially asked me not to mention his name in my writings for reasons which you will understand later on.

CHAPTER II

When I had my caravan ready the contents seemed considerable, but in fact I had only bare necessaries. In addition I took about fifty one-pound tins of Huntley & Palmer's biscuits, as these are a great delicacy to the Tibetans, especially for the lamas. I depended upon them to some extent for assistance, mostly from the head lama of the monasteries. This recognition would be of assistance, as I would be likely to be welcomed by the populace also.

I also took with me a number of silk scarves, which are the traditional ceremonial gifts in Tibet. I was informed of this courtesy previously. If you place the silk scarf around the neck of the person receiving the scarf, it is a sign that you consider him your equal. If the scarf is just handed to him he is considered beneath you.

On all occasions I remembered to place the scarf around the neck and it paid big dividends. The great lamas granted me many privileges which I accepted with open arms.

I left the small town of Kalimpong and went down into the valley of the Teesta River.

This river is considered the fastest flowing river in the world. Its colour is bluish white, caused by the melting of the snow and ice coming from the great glaciers in the Himalayas, especially the great glaciers of the mighty Kanchenjunga, the most beautiful peak of the great range of the Himalayas and considered to be more difficult to climb than Mount Everest.

The valley became deeper and deeper and the road in parts a mere track. This track is forced to follow the roaring waters of the Teesta through the gorges which have been created through the thousands of years of the waters' continuous cascading. The atmosphere on the lower levels were suffocating, and a sort of humid smell came from the thick impenetrable jungle surrounding us on all sides.

This deep green thick foilage, which it is impossible to penetrate, is filled with elephant, rhino and the ferocious Bengal tiger, and there are hundreds of other wild animals and reptiles, such as leopards, monkeys, snakes and pythons.

I was glad when I began to climb out of this dealy atmosphere. As we rose out of it, a clearing could been seen here and there, revealing majestic scenery such as the eye seldom sees.

The blue sky like a canopy covering the green foilage, with colourful rhododendron trees on sides of the mountains, while the treacherous Teesta River rushed over the jutting rocks with the roar of an express train. These scenes are still deeply printed in my memory, and I can well recall them as I write. I was fascinated by the wildness of it all; the mountains, the jungle, the river, the track, the trees and the patches of green mingling together in one beautiful yet aweinspiring panorama.

To realise that just off the track, hidden there in the jungle, might be certain death was enough to make one think, and a slip off the track into that howling torrent of the Teesta would be a terrible fate.

As one clearing after another came into view I could see the peaks of the Himalayas in the distance covered with the eternal snows, and I knew that in a day or two I must cross the pass that separates these peaks.

I was exhilarated knowing that at last I was truly on my way to the great adventure of my life, and I looked forward with joy and anticipation to what was going to happen in the future.

Chapter II

I had no fear, because I was told that all would be well with me, and I was ready to face any danger with confidence.

I knew that secreted somewhere beyond these great Himalayan mountains was the mystery I was bound to solve.

The first day we travelled twelve miles, a good day's march. We pulled up at a small village on the side of the river. Around the huts which were built on poles several feet off the gound there was a fairly large clearing with stockades where the beasts are kept at night, safe from marauding tigers and leopards. There was an official hut on the way, but this was occupied for the night, so we chose the next best thing.

I chose a small hut on the hillside, above the village; this hut was made of grass canvas, My bearer said to me, "Sahib, do you think it is safe up there?"

"Well," I replied, "it is better than down among the cattle---and others must have slept there before me, I'm sure."

The hut was about two feet from the hillside which had been cut away so that it could fit in. My bearer got out my sleeping bag, and after a wash (a basin and a pail of water had been provided for me) I had supper. Then I turned in. I had a healthy tiredness and fell off to sleep almost immediately.

During the night I was awakened by the presence of an animal between the hillside and my flimsy hut; it was obviously smelling for something and it made a growling sort of noise. I knew it was a tiger or a leopard and I must frighten it away before it got any bolder. So I took the basin full of water that I had washed in and let it fly, followed by the pail, in the direction where I thought the animal was. All this made such a hell of a noise that the beast must have got a terrific fright, for it gave a fierce growl and bolted.

Chapter II

Shortly afterwards I heard the yelling of a pig and I gathered that the beast got its meal after all---I was glad I was not the victim. In fact, though, I was not disturbed at all by this experience; I seemed rather to like it at first, but when I told my bearer the next morning he said, "Sahib, you had a very narrow escape."

I laughed it off, but at the same time I resolved to take good care to choose a more protected place the following night.

After shaving and cleaning up we had breakfast, which consisted of porridge with salt in it (porridge without salt tastes insipid to me). We had tinned cream, a piece of bacon with toast and tea. Truly I felt happy---I can almost realise that feeling as I am writing.

We started off in a very happy mood that morning, and my happiness seemed infectious, for even the animals seemed in a gay mood. We went higher and higher up the mountain track, which rose steeply for thousands of feet, and away down below I could hear the roar of the Teesta, though could not see it. I knew that part of the glaciers hundreds of miles away was in that river making its way to the sea.

"What a tale that river could tell," I said to my bearer.

"Yes," he said, "and many a life has been lost in that river, Sahib."

Part of the track had fallen away and there was barely room to pass. We clung precariously close to the inside. I was afraid that the load on the mules might touch the side and send them rolling down into the gorge a thousand feet below. Happily the muleteer was an experienced man and he led the mules past with great care. I did not chance riding my pony and walked gingerly past leading him behind me, but he also was an experienced beast---he had travelled that way may times before. Shortly after we pass I heard a rumbling noise, and there, coming down the mountainside, was a hail of boulders, some as big as the hut I had slept in on the previous night. We had just passed in time. What could have disturbed these boulders, I wondered; could it have been a mountain bear? for there were plenty around those parts, or it might have been a mountain goat.

During the rainy season, I was told, occasionally the track is impassable as the whole mountainside would fall headlong into the gorge below, and then several days would be needed to make a fresh track farther up the mountainside. Yes, it is a tricky business, climbing the Himalayas!

That night we got to the border of Sikkim, where we had comfortable accommodation in one of the well-constructed huts built by the Younghusband expedition.

A company of Gurkhas was stationed there to prevent any unauthorised person entering Sikkim, which is the gateway to Tibet. I showed my pass, signed the book, and gave all details of my expedition. On my return seven months later I signed below my previous signature to prove that I was the same person who had passed that way before and that I had got back safe and sound.

Chickens, eggs and potatoes were easily bought, and that night we had roast chicken and baked potatoes, these tasted good, for we had done a two-day journey in one day.

The following morning we crossed the river into Sikkim and made our way towards Gangtok, the capital of Sikkim. Here the political officer of Tibet, a Mr. Gould, had his residence. I had an excellent dinner with him that evening. Next I paid my respects to the Maharaja of Sikkim and we had a pleasant evening all round. His wife was a beautiful Tibetan girl, member of a highly cultured family in Yatung. She was charming and spoke English with a fascinating accent, which added to her charm.

Chapter II

Next day we started our really strenuous part of the journey, climbing up towards the Natula Pass. The track here is not more than two feet wide in most places, zig-zagging up the steep mountainside, and the higher you get the deeper the precipices and ravines become.

We passed several trains of donkeys, sometimes more than a hundred donkeys in one train, and in some trains of yaks there are eight hundred or more, carrying everything on their backs as there is no wheeled traffic in Tibet, not even a wheelbarrow. (A number of donkeys or yaks is called a train).

We met one train of donkeys on a very dangerous part, where the track is very narrow.

The outsides of the tracks are work away, the reason for this being that the animals instinctively know that if they keep near the mountainside their protruding loads might hit against jutting rocks and this could send them headlong thousands of feet over the precipice to their death, with their loads and all.

We could hear bells tinkling, bells which the donkeys carry around their necks, and we stopped at a passing place till they went by.

You can imagine what my thoughts were on my first experience of this kind.

At a night resting-place, farther along the trade route, I examined the backs of some donkeys when their loads were taken off, and I found that most of their backs were covered with sores from the rubbing of saddles on which the loads are carried. I was disgusted, to say the very least, to see how these poor little animals suffered and I remonstrated, through my interpreter, with the muleteers. They said they did not think that the donkeys felt any pain. They showed me their own feet cut by the razor-like edge of the ice that forms as the slush freezes on the track after sundown, and they did not think that the donkeys felt pain either.

When the sun is up, the snow melts on the track; but when the sun has set this slush becomes frozen with razor-like edges which crunch under your feet. Many of the Tibetans wear a sort of straw rope around their feet, and this offers some protection against the sharp edes of frozen slush.

I marvelled at the terrific loads these little donkeys with their little spindle legs carried; they struggle up the steep mountain track with a load almost equal to their own weight.

One morning, one of my mules started a kicking fit; he did not want to carry his load any farther and threw it off by kicking his heels up in the air every time we put it on. But this was soon remedied. The muleteer tied a rope round the mule's feet from the back foot to the corresponding front foot, and when the mule kicked again he fell flat on his nose; he did not kick anymore and we continued on our journey. Apparently it was not the first time this trick had been tried.

Slowly we wound our way up the steep Himalayas and in two days we reached the top of the Natula Pass, covered with the eternal snows. This is about 2,000 feet above the wood line, about 16,000 feet above sea level---a sight I shall never forget. Away in the distance, as far as the eye could see, were the majestic peaks of the mighty Himalayas covered with snow. I looked away above and beyond, and away down towards the Chumbi Valley. Here was a strange land, strange that is to the ouside world and which the outside world was stranger. It was like a land of dreams, and my heart thrilled at the magnificent sight, knowing that down there, the valley would mean another step towards the fulfilment of my life-long desire.

25

Chapter II

As we reached lower down towards the Chumbi Valley the mountainside was covered with rhododendron trees in full bloom, some pink, some red, some purple, some white, and the floor of the green valley, 11,000 feet above sea level, was coloured with wild flowers. Here and there you could see the red-topped Tibetan houses, surrounded by a patchwork of cultivated land, some patches green, some red, some brown, and through the centre flows the rushing Amo Chu River, the waters of which are turned into channels to irrigate the land. I stood enraptured, gazing upon a scene unparalleled anywhere in the world.

As I looked upon this emerald green valley coloured as it was with wild flowers and dotted here and there with the red roofs of the houses surrounded with a patchwork of cultivated land, threaded by a rushing river, and all this surrounded on all sides by towering snow-clad mountains, I saw wrapped in the midst, secluded in the mountainside a mysterious Tibetan monastery, a school of mystery, where knowledge of a forgotten age still existed. It looked for all the world like a crazy carpet that one could look upon for hours without being tired for the looking.

We rested for the night at a comfortable hut on the mountainside. The following day we would wend our way down into Yatung.

The Natula Pass we had just crossed separated us now from the outside world. We were now in the land of mystery, the forbidden land on the roof of the world.

It is true that one finds what one is seeking. Some seek pictures of the beautiful, the rugged, the dangerous. I was not seeking pictures; I was seeking something eternal and I knew I would find it.

Chapter II

A fire was made up in my hut and I sat before it, thinking deeply what the morrow would bring. I must have sat for a considerable time, for the fire was now low.

I put out the candlelight and went to bed. As the red glow of the fire grew dimmer I was startled out of my reverie. Close behind me a figure appeared at my bedside. I thought my bearer had returned for something and I said, "What do you want, bearer?"

There was no answer. I looked again and saw that it was a person robed like a lama. I felt a tingling through my body; I looked at the face and saw that it was a very fine Mongolian type, a high brow, with piercing eyes, his face lit up as if the sun was shining from it. His eyes were set well apart and the face was beautifully formed. I saw his lips move but could not hear what he said; he smiled a smile as of one who knew, and gradually he disappeared from view.

I am not in the habit of having hallucinations, nor imagining things, for I have a very searching mind and do not accept things without due consideration. This indeed must have been a visitation of some kind and I knew that the morrow would give me the answer.

On reaching Yatung the following day I was met again by my friend. I call him "my friend," in fact he was more than a friend to me, now. I told him of my experience, but he said nothing about it.

He said, "You will rest here tonight and tomorrow I want you to meet someone who knows you."

I was puzzled at this remark, for I could hardly know anyone in this forbidden land.

When the next day arrived I was deeply interested in the person I was going to meet.

Chapter II

We started out alone, just the two of us, and I asked, "How far have we to go to meet this person who knows me?"

He pointed up the valley and said, "There is Lingmatang. There is a master there whom I want you to meet, the one who knows you. He lives in the monastery, though he has long ago passed by their beliefs and dogmas and ritual, but it suits him to stay there. He is reverenced by all lamas, in fact throughout the whole of the land, as a great Master. Yet he will tell you, it is not a master you need, for that which is greatest is within yourself, and there, only, will you find the answer to what you seek."

After this he became silent and no further words were spoken until we reached the monastery.

The monastery was cunningly situated in the mountain-side and I did not see it until I was right there. A more inspiring sight is seldom seen. We came upon it all at once. I wondered how such a massive stone structure could have been built on the side of the mountain and which it stood.

I stood for a minute, wondering deeply what was in store for me. After climbing the huge rock steps we reached the massive door of the monastery, which must have been at least thirty feet high. The huge door swung open silently as if the hinges were on ball-bearings.

Apparently they must have seen us and were expecting us, for we were immediately attended by several lamas, who led us through several halls into a winding passage until we reached a door panelled in gold. At the side hung a long piece of brocade to which was attached a golden tassel. When one of the lamas conducting us pulled it, I could hear a gong sounding in the inside.

Chapter II

Then the door opened and we entered, and there stood before me the great Geshi Rimpoche himself, the very face I saw two nights before in the hut. I could not take my eyes off him. This meeting had a tremendous effect on me and I realised that at that moment I was on the verge of a great mystery. He welcomed me as his brother, and a warm feeling immediately went through me. I knew that I had felt this influence before, yes, for a long time, it must have been for several years.

I felt extremely happy and we talked about my journey and the world I had come from, for he himself had travelled all over the world and could speak several languages.

Little more was said and we adjourned for some food which was already prepared for us. I was shown my comfortable quarters and told that I needed rest and tomorrow we would speak together again. Needless to say I slept as I had never slept before.

On the following morning my friend, Geshi Rimpoche and myself, the three of us, walked slowly among the wild flowers, until we came to a secluded spot beside a stream where the water gently slid over the polished rock, polished through the ages by the continuous flow of the silent stream of water.

The air was electric. Geshi Rimpoche spoke about his visit to me in the hut.

He said, "You know that astral projection is very easy in this atmosphere."

"Yes," I replied, "but that is not the first time you have visited me. The same influence I have sensed for many years. Now I understand."

Chapter II

My words seemed to flow very easily, for I felt a sense of complete contentment, and I said, "What I want to know is why I have been singled out for this work."

He answered, "My son, for this you were born," and he continued in a voice that I could listen to forever: "To a great extent our desires are often the will of the Creator and all the forces of Heaven and earth are brought into action to express that will. A higher power had the planning of your being here now."

He was silent for a minute. Then he said, "Did you plan your coming on this earth?"

I replied, "It is believed by some that reincarnation is a truth, you know."

"Ah," he said, "now you have accepted what another has told you or what you read in books, but you do not know whether it is true or not, nor does it matter! There can only be 'One' Life and Life is not divided; the Life that is in you and me must be the same Life, there can be no separation in the Life that is 'One'. This Life in the body, you will find, is the same Life beyond the body, the totality of all Life cannot be separated in you or me.

"There can be no separation even in what you see and feel! Matter is a name you have given to the material world, but do you know what it is? When you try to find out what it is, it changes into something else, and when you try to find what that something else is, it changes into something else, and this goes on *ad infinitum.* There is no finality; there is no finality in Infinity. The mind can never know 'Truth' which is beyond the mind; the mind can only create an idea of Truth, an image of Truth, a belief in regard to Truth, but this is obviously not Truth Itself. Therefore you will never know what Truth is, but you will know that Truth *is,* and only within yourself can Truth be found."

Chapter II

I said, "I know that very well now. There is a mass of books in circulation telling us what Truth is. Now I can see that those who wrote these books are, themselves, just searching for that which they do not know. All they have is but ideas, words, that create an endless stream of further ideas and words."

"That is true, my son," he said, "but they have their value. It shows that they have begun to think for themselves and their value to others is of a similar nature." "But your work," he continued, "is to show what an idea is, what an image is; to show: that which is made up in the mind is not Truth. But you must have an idea first before you can understand what an idea is. You yourself were filled with ideas which you thought were the Truth. But that which you made up in your mind is not Truth, because Truth is not made up, and you will hear that again and again.

"Yes," I said, "I know that now, and I would be the last one to condemn another for having ideas."

"Yes," he went on, "But there are those who will condemn you for not having an idea or image of the Truth, though you know very well that an idea or an image is not the Truth, for the Truth is neither an idea nor an image.

These things are mental creations, but the Truth is not created. Truth is the creativeness behind all Creation. Yet that which is created is not Truth, only the Uncreated is creative, and that is the Truth. 'I am the Truth, I am the Life," the Master Jesus said. It is the same for you and for us all, for there is but 'One' in all, and all in 'One'."

He had just finished when the *chonghas* (ceremonial trumpets) sounded calling the lamas to prayer.

I said, "Then do you condemn all this form and ritual?"

"No," he replied, "if I condemned it I could not understand it, but now that I understand what it is I no longer take part in it. The Christian religion has form and ritual too. It may be slightly different but they are all similar.

"Ritual is mental, not spiritual; the ways of performing it may be different, but it is all of the mind and this is what you have to understand, otherwise you can never be free. If you refuse to understand it, you are still bound by it, whether you believe it or disbelieve it.

Spirituality is the silent expression of Love, Wisdom and Power, not the repeating of ritual.

"Now we will go in and take part in the ceremony so that you can understand it, and also for the experience; then you will see that all religions are similar. The words may be different , the chanting may be different, but the mind is following an idea, that is all. But it is not the Truth that sets you free. You can only be free when you understand what the mind if made up of, and how and from where it is made up.

"Why are some Buddhist, and others Christian, why are some Mohammedans, and others atheists? Are they not fundamentally all the same? They may be different religions, but they follow an ideal, and so does the atheist. Believing and not believing is the same thing; it is all in the mind, is it not? It is but the conflict of ideas."

The *chonghas* kept sounding with their long booming tones, like the boom of a giant gong.

"Now," he said, "you have bells instead of *chonghas*, calling your people to prayer."

We entered the great hall where all the lamas were now sitting lotus-fashion, chanting *Om Mani Padme Hum* which means, "Hail the jewel in the lotus flower!" When one section would end on the *"Hum"* the other section would begin with the *"Om,"* so there was a continuous sound which caused even the great pillars of the temple hall to vibrate. At intervals the great gongs would be sounded, their heavy booming tones vibrating and mingling with many little bells as the voices of the lamas grew louder and louder.

The effect it had on me was that I felt I was going into a deep trance as the sound vibrated through my brain.

I could understand now how some of the lamas became ascetics through the repeating of the words *Om Mani Padme Hum;* it was a matter of self-hypnosis.

After the service was over I said I was greatly affected by the power of the sound of the chanting, the gongs and the *chonghas.*

"Yes," said my friend, "the lamas may know the power of sound, but if they knew the source of it, they could lead the world. The Spirit alone has voice, you know," and he said no more.

These were the first words he uttered that day.

"Now, come and we will enjoy some music of the early masters and some of the latest too," said Rimpoche.

I could see that Rimpoche wanted to relieve the tension, for this day was a very wonderful one for me, and I was still caught up with the many things I had seen and heard. The Master knew his pupil, as all great Masters do. So we adjourned into his inner sanctuary where he kept a magnificent gramophone with a perfect tone.

We partook of a light meal and listened to the music of the great masters, of Beethoven, Wagner, Grieg, Mozart, Bach, Mendelssohn, Chopin and others.

Chapter II

After this we retired each to his own quarters.

I started the outcropping of my mind, watching, observing what was rising to the surface impersonally. It was not long before I grasped, "That which the mind is made up of is not the Truth."

Eventually, there was a silence, not a silence that I was accustomed to, but a silence that came from a mind that was freed from conflicting ideas and images. And in that Silence I experienced a sense of Reality. In that "moment" was Eternity, and all the power and glory of Its expression was *"Now."*

If I could only hold this tremendous source of wisdom, love and power! But then I started thinking and lost it.

I tried to recapture it that moment but it was gone, it was now an experience, a memory, the moment that was past was no more. Yet I did not realise that in that moment was the Eternal, and to live from moment to moment was the Living Truth, the Oneness of all things was Now. There was no beginning and no ending. When I realised this I was no longer in separation. I was one with all, the Creator and His Creation became one with me.

Words cannot explain or reveal this state of Being, it was mine now and forever, and I was satisfied; the search was over, and now I could go further. I knew that nothing outside myself could reveal It, I had to realise It for myself.

I stayed in my own quarters for the remainder of the day, and in the evening I passed off into a peaceful sleep.

Next morning I felt light, as if a great burden had been taken from me. I lived in the moment of Eternity, I was no longer anxious, my craving ceased. I was free.

Chapter II

I went outside, the sky was clear, the stars were still gleaming and sparkling like thousands of diamonds set in a dark blue canopy lighting up the mountains and valley in relief.

Gradually the sun began to creep up from behind the great mountains covered with snow, and the colour display was a panorama of beauty. The twinkling of the stars gave way to the rays of the rising sun, the dark blue canopy faded into a light blue reflecting all the shades of the dazzling colours of the rainbow--- firstly, a dull red with streams of light bursting amid the edges, then the red and pink would come into view, intermingling with each other, spreading rays in all directions reflected from the snowclad mountains piercing the blue sky, while the shadows dissolved away in the valley below.

As the first rays of the sun came into view they lit up the portals of the monastery and I could hear the lamas chanting *Om Mani Padme Hum* which was echoing down the valley, with the incense wafting on the gentle breeze. My senses were forming an indelible picture that has withstood the millions of impressions gathered since. And as it comes into my mind I can see before me now that most exhilarating sight and feel the exhilarating atmosphere and hear the sounds of the rushing river and booming of the great gong, the sounding of the *chonghas,* the chanting of the lamas and the enchanting aroma of incense. Yes, it was unforgettable, to say the least.

I was gazing into space, I don't know for how long. As I turned I saw my friend just behind me, doing the same thing.

"I see you are enjoying the splendour, my son."

"Yes," I said, "I feel entirely different in this atmosphere."

"Yes," he said, "since every thought wave creates a different motion in the atoms and cells of the body the facial muscles reveal the expression of the thought waves and I see that you have become younger, my son. The beat of your heart and your breathing have already revealed a change in your functional oganism. Cause and effect are one, my son."

I listened attentively to his words because I wanted to understand everything he said.

This was important and I knew he could read my mind.

"Yes, my son, the Divine Creation is the transformation of the Eternal Ever-present Intelligent Energy into form, emanating from the Divine Mind and changing into greater splendour according to your capacity to receive. Vibration is the keynote of creation and the rhythmic organisation of atoms into the pattern we see before us."

"It will," he continued, "maintain health and strength in mind and body, and Its magnetic attraction and inherent intelligent action can be used for higher purposes and greater accomplishments that will yet stagger the imagination of man. Not only does this intelligent action manifest itself in the individual but it also rushes beyond the confines of the individual in ever-widening circles to envelop the whole earth's circumference, and according to the Divine Law of 'Love your neighbour as yourself' we will reflect the beauty of the Divine in our own souls and those who come after us will manifest a greater expression of the Divine Nature that created us by the Word that was in the beginning---the Christ of God behind and within all mankind."

He stopped for a minute and there was a silence.

Then he said to me, in a subdued voice, "You know that Geshi Rimpoche is leaving his earthly body for good soon, that is why we desired you to see him in the flesh. He looks comparatively young, but he has passed through over two hundred years of constant work for the world at large, yet the world does not know him. Here he comes now," and when I looked at him he did not seem to be more than fifty years of age. His very presence rejuvenated me.

He must have sensed what we were saying, for he said in no uncertain way, "Yes, the intelligence that created all you see is ever-present, and, when man prepares himself for Its true expression, through man will come things that we can yet only dimly dream about. Yes," he went on, "the same Intelligence that is active throughout the whole Universe is active here and now. The only deterrent to Its expression is man himself, yet through man will come things that will stagger the imagination. Man is the focal point through which it can manifest, and how mighty is Its omnipotence, waiting to reveal Its Omnipresent Omniscience!

"Life does not end when we leave the body, there is no division or separation in the Life in the body and the totality of all Life in the Universe, *It is one,* and so-called death does not divide or separate It." And there was a deep Silence which we all felt.

CHAPTER III

On looking down on the green plains of the Chumbi Valley I saw a large number of yaks grazing. They were grazing in the morning mist, for the grass is sweeter when the dew is on it.

It seemed a familiar scene to me, though in a strange land. In the Highlands of Scotland in the early morning mists I used to watch the Highland cattle grazing, and sometimes there were wild deer which had come down in the early morning to graze in the green pastures. The first thing I used to look for when I got up was to see if there were any wild deer down from the hills. And here was a similar scene, for the yaks is an animal with shaggy hair not unlike the Highland cattle, with the exception that the yak has a hump where the neck and shoulders meet.

I asked, "Whom do all these yaks belong to, I did not see them there last night?"

"Look over to the side of the river," replied Rimpoche, "and you will see a large pile of wool bales. That is a yak train of about four hundred, I would say, carrying Tibetan wool to India. It is quite a common event here. When they have had their morning feed the teamsters will gather them together and load them up for the next day's trek over the pass. Let us go down amongst them, it will be an experience for you."

So we walked down to the floor of the valley and sure enough there were about eight hundred bales of Tibetan wool. Each yak carries two bales, one on each side of its saddle.

Tibetan wool is eagerly sought in India because of its fine texture.

"The history of the yak is a very interesting one," said Rimpoche, "for they supply all the needs of the Tibetans. The hair is woven into great tents in which the nomads live. The pelts are used to make boots and shoes, the flesh is eaten for food, and the butter and the milk supply is more than ample. A great deal of butter is used in lamps, especially in the monasteries, and some lamps are kept burning continuously. Yak dung is gathered and used to make fires, to cook the food and to heat the houses. The yaks are also used for ploughing the lands and they carry everything on their backs that the Tibetan needs. So, you see, the yak is the most useful animal in Tibet and there are hundreds of them roaming wild in the plains.

"There are valleys in Tibet where no living person has ever been and there are also valleys in Tibet where people live and no one knows anything about them; neither do they know anything about what is outside. The live in a world of their own, hemmed in by the great mountains, and they have made little or no effort to know what is beyond.

"In my travels into these isolated parts, I came upon a monastery where the Bon-Bon worship was still in operation, and on rare occasions human sacrifices are practised. The lamas have stamped most of this devil-worship out in Tibet and, though steeped in religion, dogmas and superstition themselves, they have at least done this one real service to the country."

"Yes," I said, "I would like to see more and hear more about the monasteries and lamas; they interest the outside world a lot, and weird tales have been circulated about them."

"Yes," said Rimpoche, "wherever you have dogma and superstition at its height you will find ignorance and poverty among the people. This is undoubtedly a great hinderance to progress. Wherever you find religious superstition, the people are poor, because they are prayed to, prayed for and preyed upon, and as long as they can be kept ignorant the better it is for those who rule through superstition and fear. But this is fast coming to an end. Even in Tibet, the most remote country in the world, there are those who are beginning to think things out for themselves."

"Do you know," he continued, "that there are over three thousand monasteries in Tibet - the largest being Drepung which is situated near Lhasa and has over nine thousand lamas in it.

These lamaseries are like cities; they are completely self-contained. The next largest is Seara, not far from Drepung with over eight thousand lamas.

"Ganden Monastery which is beyond Lhasa has about five thousand lamas. This is the great centre of learning in Tibet and here flock the ablest of the student lamas. I taught in this monastery for years."

"That is interesting," I remarked, "what do they teach there?"

"They teach philosophy, mysticism and magic, astrology and the study of ancient literature and metaphysics, healing and other studies. There are some very great Tibetan scholars and mystics there as well as those who work magic, and I intend that you shall meet some of them."

The oldest monastery in Tibet is Samye. This monastery was founded by the wizard lama Padma-Samb-Hava some hundreds of years ago. The legend about this wizard lama is that he caused the spirits of the Malgro lake nearby to bring in a great quantity of gold and precious stones which were secreted in the vaults hewn out of the great rock upon which the monastery is built. These vast stores of gold and precious stones have been kept there intact for several hundred years.

"My own opinion," said Rimpoche, "is that Padma-Samb-Hava made the lamas dig in the mountains for gold and search the lake nearby for precious stone, for this area is considered the richest in the whole of Tibet. Anyone finding gold and precious stones must bring them to the monastery; to keep them for themselves would be sacrilege. So you can see why the monasteries are so wealthy and the people so poor. People are told what to think and how to think and what to do, and only comparatively few are able to think for themselves and gain freedom."

"It is much the same in the West," I said.

"Yes," he affirmed, "people are seeking the truth while living in the false, but the false will remain till they see the false, then the false will cease to be. The false can never contain the truth, ignorance does not contain understanding."

I could see at once that Rimpoche had passed into a state of inspiration and I would not interrupt by asking any more questions. So we sat and listened to this ancient sage full of wisdom and truth, and I was filled with a longing to seek deeper into the Reality of things and as I listened I felt what he was saying had a transforming effect upon me.

"They cannot see the false," he said, "because they are caught up in it. They are conditioned by their prejudices, by their belief, and what others tell them. They have failed to assert their creative faculty of discerning that which is not true. The only truth about the false is that it is false and they will still be caught up in it till they understand it, and how they have been caught up in it."

Now he took on the role of the teacher. "I want you to see this clearly, my son," he said, looking at me, "otherwise you will retain the false, hoping to see the Truth. But it cannot be done."

"Firstly," he said, "you must see what makes you believe in anything, then you will see what makes you antagonistic to another belief, or idea, or people. If you came here conditioned by your own

42

opinions, then you will see only through that conditioning, but if you are free from your own conditioning you can see us free from ours. Then you will see me as I see you, stripped of all form, all nationalities, all religions and creeds. Then we will know each other to be made in the image and likeness of our Creator, made out of the same Substance, the same Life, and having the 'One' Consciousness within, for there cannot be any division, God being infinite in nature, there can only be God, there can be nothing else and this is our Being."

I breathed a sigh, for here was the secret of the brotherhood of man and the Fatherhood of God, and he put it in such a few words. I did not move, nor did I reply one way or another, I must not break the spell, I thought. His eyes were closed now, his face took on an angelic look as if a great angel messenger was speaking through him, and it could be so, through one who knew the inner secrets of Life. He continued in that beautiful mellow tone of his and every sentence stood clearly out by itself.

"You organize yourselves into separate groups of religions, of nationalities, of ideologies, each believing that what you stand for is the real thing. So you wrangle with one another and when wrangling cannot solve the problem you butcher one another. Now is there any Truth in that?"

I felt myself saying, "No," but my tongue was tied. I felt a deep feeling within me and it was coming to the surface. Something was preventing me from uttering a single word.

"You are afraid because you do not understand. So you want a guide, you want a belief, so you are further caught up in the conflict, and because you are in conflict you are afraid. So you want an ideal so that you can look at your fear, but this only covers up your fear while you do not understand. When you understand your fear, you are freed from your fear, then your conflict will disappear.

Chapter III

"Your ideals and your fears are made up in your mind, and what is made up in your mind is unreal, so both your ideal and your fears have no foundation in Truth.

"Truth is not made up in the mind, Truth *Is!* You do not make it up! What is made up, is not Truth!

"You can see the false as you discern your relationship with people, ideas and things. If there is antagonism, if there is fear, if there is craving, prejudice or conflict, there can be no relationship.

"As long as the mind is in conflict blaming, resisting, condemning, there can be no understanding, no relationship with one another. It is obvious you must not condemn if you want to understand.

"When you see the false you will know it, you will no longer be part of it, and then the True comes into being, because It always *Is,* It is Real and Eternal and everpresent, moment to moment, never changing. It is only your mind that changes from one idea to another. When you know what a belief is, what an ideal is, then the mind will free itself, and in that freedom there is the Real.

"It is so important to understand that the mind is made dull through condemning, through blaming, through avoidance, through acceptance and through resistance. Only in your relationship, freed from all conditioning is there freedom, and in this freedom there is peace, and in peace there is Love.

"If you are filled with likes and dislikes you are merely projecting your own conditioning."

I thought for a moment how true that is, for the other person is but a mirror in which we see ourselves.

Chapter III

"You will see some so-called pleasant and unpleasant things as you pass through Tibet," he said, "but if the unpleasant upsets you, you are resisting, you are not free. When there is Love we observe the facts but they do not repel us. I know you have the capacity for this Love, otherwise you would not be here, my son.

"Some repeat words---mantrims, these things do not fill the heart. On the contrary they empty the heart of whatever it has. The heart can only be filled when the mind is not fabricating. When the mind is not caught up in opposites, in ideas, prejudice and the like, then only is the heart alive with Love.

"Then one knows what it is to have that warmth, the richness in holding the hand of another. Love being perfect in its own Eternity knows no resistance, no opposition, neither will you fear any more, because you will be filled with Eternal Love, for God is Love, and He alone exists. That which hides Him is but a mental fabrication. Now I know that the false is falling away from you, my son. It is said in Isaiah 65; 17, 'For behold, I create new heavens and a new earth: and the former shall not be remembered, nor come into mind.'"

With these last words he opened his eyes, in them there was a far-away look. I could see that soon he would dissolve his earthly body into the substance from which it arose, for he was truly in the mind of God, his Spirit was freed from all desires, all craving for both Spiritual and material had ceased, he knew he was Life, he had found "*Being.*"

He rose, gathered his robes about him and went away.

I was left to myself for the remainder of the day. Both Rimpoche and my friend purposely left me. I knew it was for the purpose of letting me work things out for myself. For on several occasions I would ask a question and all I would get would be a vacant look. I know now how stupid those questions were, but I did not think so at the time, for they were of great importance to me then. But now I have the same habit; when people ask me a lot of question, it may seem rude not to answer but no rudeness is implied, only deep Love rules the heart, knowing that an answer would only mean another image.

Perhaps you are also grasping the fact, my dear reader; if an answer were given it would merely create another idea which would only hinder and not help to free the mind from its own formulations, beliefs, prejudices and fears.

Facts are facts, but a fact is not a belief nor is a belief a fact. When facts are seen as facts, not a belief in a fact, then there is understanding.

A scientific question can be answered, or, at least, the way of finding out facts can be taught. But the belief in a fact is not the fact itself, for a belief in a fact can never reveal the fact.

When I saw this clearly I stopped asking questions.

I must have been sitting by myself for hours. My mind was emptying itself out; I could watch my thoughts as if they were pictures on a screen, quite impersonally. I was beginning to understand now what my mind was made up of. I neither judged, praised nor condemned; it was as if I were observing the mind of another.

Then the deeper stratas of the mind were giving up its cherished ideas, things that I had held fast to were being loosened one after another. I could see clearly now how and from where my mind was made up. It was the result of hereditary tendencies, countless thousands of impressions, ideas, prejudices, most of them being received from the opinions and suggestions and statements of those who were caught up in their own conditioning, caught up in the false, which prevented them from seeing the Truth of the only "One" in which there was no division.

I could also see how I accepted without question or examination; thus I was conditioned.

I could now see that I could live in the false without condemning and without being affected by it, because I knew how it all came about, and I resolved I would never again be caught up in it, even should I be surrounded by it on all sides.

I could see why I must be aware, wide-awake in questioning the opinion of others. I could now search their statements with the speed of lightning and realise that they were merely imitators, they were merely gramophones.

Yet I knew that was not enough; I must question my own thought-feeling-reaction to see where it was moving, what was moving it and why. What was the motive behind it?

I could now understand what was in my mind, and could see from where it arose, and by seeing this clearly I was freed from its blinding effects. It did not matter very much now whether it was true or not. The words of my friend came to me so clearly and I understood now as I never understood before, "It does not matter very much whether it is true or not!"

I could see how the light was shown on the path which I must move along by myself, for no one else could reveal the Truth to me. I had to find It out alone, and I saw how important this was. It was my own now, not the idea of another, for the truth of another could never be my truth. If it did it would be merely an idea, a belief, and I would still be bound. How clearly I saw this now, that I must experience the Truth by myself. I understood the way I was being shown how to move along under my own guidance, that guidance of the Spirit that is Eternal and Ever-present within me "NOW."

I saw that this moment was Eternal. I could only "Be," each moment. The moment just past became a memory, to try to recapture it would merely be a mental image. I must live each moment to be free from the past or the future. I could see that both the past and the future only existed in the mind and nowhere else. "Now" was the only Reality. I was the Life Eternal, I could be nothing else, anything else would merely be an idea, a self-created image.

I was becoming consciously free and I experienced a power that was beyond the mind. I was the focal point through which the All-ness of the Universal Power could manifest. My faith was no longer the opposite of fear. It was now a knowing, for I had experienced Reality.

Although I do not know what It is I know that It is, and there is nothing else but It, therefore I am It to. "I and the Father are one."

I could sense the power of the Master, "It was the Father who ever remained within me," He was the operator, and there was nothing now to prevent this power from acting. I had only to be conciously aware, and through this awareness, only, could Reality be expressed.

I thought, how did I ever miss this wonderful thing, this knowing? It was so simple, and I could discern now how I had been caught up in separation, in belief. I was separated from my fellows by my ideas, my beliefs, my prejudices, my fears. I could see it all now. I knew that the Real Self within was the same in each and every one---and now I knew, really knew. It was no longer a platitude or a mere saying, what I did to another I did to myself,

Chapter III

"Whatever you do unto one of these so you do unto Me," did it unto Him who sent me, for I was in the Whole and the Whole was in me.

I could never go back now. I actually felt within myself that freedom, that wisdom and love, that is all power in heaven and earth.

I knew now the healing power of the Master and I felt also at that moment that I could say, "Arise and walk," and it became so, for throughout the world, ever since, I have healed thousands of people, some whom I have never seen. Age has disappeared from me and my youthful appearance mystifies everyone who knows my age.

It sounds like a great romance but it is greater than any romance ever known. Yet all have the same power, and the only thing that is preventing Its manifestation is, because It is covered up with the false, with separation, not only between man and man but also between man and God through a belief in separation, yet we are "One" in Reality. It is this that the ignorant cannot see yet.

Good and evil, I saw, were relative, a fabrication of the mind, for there could be no evil in the Divine which alone was Real, Eternal and Ever-present. I could see the falseness of the preaching about evil, hell and the devil which exists today, how people are caught up in the evil and can see nothing else. What the mind sees, so must that mind be likewise, is true in fact.

Yes, the teachings of the Master Jesus are covered up with sanctimonious formalities by those who profess him, they mystify themselves and confuse the people.

I know now that this book could not have been written before. There is a time for everything, and the time has now come for this great story to be told.

Chapter III

I was brought out of my reverie, again, by the sound of the *chonghas*, the ceremonial trumpets calling the lamas to prayer. The sun was now setting behind the mountain into which the monastery was built. The magnificent colour display was something never to be forgotten; from pinks to dark reds with rays spreading in all directions, the monastery nestled in it as if in a great fire.

I made my way back to the monastery and my friend and Geshi Rimpoche came to meet me. I must have had a radiant look about me for my friend said, "You have regained your youth, my son." It was true, for I felt it, felt as if the burdens of thousands of years of inherited conditioning had slipped away from me. I was free, with a freedom I cannot explain.

Words have no meaning to describe the ecstasy of that freedom and the power that it gave me. That evening we listened to more music of the classics. It was my medicine and I knew it.

The following day I wanted to tour the monastery. I now wanted to see the images in gold and silver, some studded with precious stones, about which I had heard so much.

I was conducted by one of the lamas called Tsong Sen who could speak English well; he was not more than twenty-five years old. He had been educated at an English school in Darjeeling. Yet his desire to become a lama brought him back to Tibet.

"I am fortunate in being able to speak English, which gives me the honour of conducting you through our monastery," he said.

"It is a great pleasure to have you," I thanked him, for indeed it was a pleasure for me to have a guide who could speak English well.

We first went into a room where some of the head lamas were having tea and I was asked to partake tea with them. I considered it an honour because of the fact that their sanctum is very secluded, but when they heard that I was a pupil of Geshi Rimpoche they were delighted to have me. I knew beforehand what the tea would be like, though I had not really tasted it before.

Their tea comes from China in the form of a solid reddish brick, this is scraped into an urn, into which is put a piece of rancid butter and some salt. Then boiling water is poured on to it and allowed to simmer for hours. The taste to me was more like castor oil, which I disliked intensely, having been given castor oil once every week when I was a boy.

In the ordinary way lamas dwell over their tea talking on many subjects relative to the monastery, and they take sips of tea now and then; this goes on for hours. When I tasted it I nearly vomited, but I could not show my dislike of their wonderful tea, so I gulped it down quickly, trying not to taste the rancid butter and salt as it passed down my throat. I was very glad when that was over, but as soon as I put down my cup it was filled up again. I had not bargained for that. I now sipped it very, very slowly so that there was always some tea in the cup, knowing now that this would prevent them from filling it up again. Yet after some time I grew to like their tea; it had a stimulating effect upon me and helped to keep out the cold. I took my departure from the abbot's sanctuary and was conducted by my guide who explained the many interesting things to me.

He said, "You will have noticed that the monastery is always built with its portals facing the rising sun. The face must be along the front edge of the rock and the back against the mountain itself, which protects it."

"The site," he continued, "is chosen by an astrologer and the day fixed for the laying of the foundation stone, and every year afterwards a ceremony is carried out to commemorate the foundation, no matter if hundreds of years have passed and some monasteries are 1,000 years old. Charms, sacred books, gold and silver images of great value are also laid in the foundation."

I said, "There will be a good haul some day for someone in the distant future when all this kind of business is done away with."

He looked at me in astonishment and I could see that his English education had not changed his fixed ideas.

We came to the library. "Now," he said, "this library is one of the most famous and ranks with Ganden for its rare and ancient manuscripts. The printing of these ancient manuscripts is done with large wooden type on a long piece of rough paper which takes up an immense amount of room."

I could see hundreds of these shelves packed with this large bulky printed matter which was attended by a number of lamas. Here and there scattered around the library were lamas busy reading, taking no heed of us. The room itself was as big as an average town hall. In the entrance to the main hall were images about twelve feet high draped with gold brocade and silk scarves. These images, he said, were the protectors to prevent evil spirits from entering in.

"You don't believe that would stop them, do you?" I asked.

No answer!

In the inner rooms or sanctuaries there were golden and silver images in glass cases, and hundreds of gold and silver butter lamps were burning in front of the altar. They were filled with yak butter and the wick stayed alight as long as the butter lasted, and in some cases those lamps were kept burning continually for hundreds of years.

He explained that their religion taught about the many different hells of torment. There seemed to be a hell for every type of person;

even doctors who kill their patients had a hell of their own, where they were dissected again and again and then put together afterwards. Black lines are drawn over the body to guide the devil with his red hot saw. There is also a hell for busybodies, where their tongues are split into several parts from the root to the tip, then hot skewers are pierced through them. Those who grumble have hot molten lead poured down their throats.

In some of the hells there are icebergs; the victim is thrown into a great crevasse and left there to be crushed as the ice walls pounded him to dust.

"No wonder," I said, "the poor Tibetan is afraid when you teach him all this sort of stuff. Surely you do not believe it, do you?"

"Not really," he said in a sort of half-believing way, "but we are told to teach it to the people."

"Surely," I exclaimed, "you are all hypocrites. Why don't you tell them the truth?"

"We would not have any power in the land," he replied.

"Then," I said, "there must be a hell for you too." He took on a look of astonishment.

I added: "I suppose there is a hell for those who do not give to the monastery, so you can make them give through fear."

"Yes, of course," he said.

"Don't you think it will backfire one day? Tibet will not always be the isolated country it is today. Surely the great scholar-lamas do not believe in all this rubbish?"

"No," he said, "there are great mystics among the lamas, great scholars, healers and prophets, scientists, atomic scientists, who know more about the atom than you do in the West.

When you go to Ganden you will meet some of these scholars; they will also amaze you with the knowledge they have of the outside world."

"I have heard of them, You know I am a pupil of the great Geshi Rimpoche."

"Yes," he replied, "the name 'Rimpoche' means precious one. He is a master of masters."

I said, "Why do you not ask him to teach you?"

"He is not taking any more pupils now, unfortunately; but I hope to be a pupil of Geshi Thudru. His name means Master of Wisdom. He was also a teacher in Ganden Monastery."

"I am going to meet him soon," I told my guide, adding: "Still, you know of the falseness of your teaching, and yet you keep on teaching it to hold your people bound by superstition."

"Yes," he said, "but you do the same in the West. Look at the massive buildings you have. Money spent on stone, mortar and regalia, and other things that could help thousands of poor people."

I pointed out: "But you have to educate people first. I saw that when certain people were given houses with baths they kept their coal in them." I added: "Our people also believe in sacrifice, which is merely a form of exploitation. There is not much difference---you may be a little more crude but it is much the same after all."

I could see that my softening-up process was having an effect.

"Yes," he said, "unfortunately it is true. Most people are still caught up in superstition and fear."

"But it is fast crumbling away," I said.

We then came to the wheel of life, which depicted the endless birth, death and rebirth of man.

I said, "This is a Hindu philosophy is it not?"

He had it off pat and related how and why man is born again and again.

I said, "You go round the country teaching *this* to the people!"

I could see that he did not yet have the knowledge and understanding of the false, and he was a bit upset. So I did not talk to him any more about it. I could see why Geshi Rimpoche did not take him as a pupil.

He told me the story of how he first went to Rimpoche and asked to become a chela.

Rimpoche took him down to the river and asked him to kneel down and put his face on the surface of the water. Then Rimpoche pushed his head under the water and kept it there until he struggled violently to get up. When Rimpoche let him up he asked him what he wanted most when his head was under the water and he replied, "My breath."

Then said Rimpoche, "When you want the Truth as much as you wanted your breath, come back to me."

It was interesting to see the many hundreds of images, many of them of gigantic size, usually dressed in gold brocade of great value and draped with silken scarves.

Chapter III

When I got back I spoke to Rimpoche about all this, and he gave me a clear picture of the whole thing.

He said, "There are two distinct sects of lamas in Tibet, the red and the yellow. The yellow follow the mystic side, and it is what I studied. The other follow the ritual and ceremony; they like the outside shows and parades. They do not display any mystic powers like those of the yellow. The Ganden Monastery is distinctly yellow and there I studied and taught for some years.

I said, "It would be just as difficult to speak to Tsong Sen, the lama who conducted me, about the Truth as it would be to speak to a bishop or a professor of theology."

He laughed loudly at this and said, "It is remarkable how quickly they throw off the yoke when it is put to them in the right way."

I told him I tried it with a professor of theology in the West but it did not work.

"Try again and you may now succeed," he said.

Then he added, "Tsong Sen's people are wealthy people and he is able to have a room of his own where his friends can come to see him."

"What about the poorer lamas?" I asked.

"Oh, they sleep together in one of the large dormitories."

"And he sleeps in a room by himself?" I asked.

"Yes," was the reply, "you see his people subscribe generously to the monastery. It is the way of the country. There are set divisions as you are already aware, and only time will change them."

Chapter III

Geshi Rimpoche told me that nearly every family sends one male member to be a lama.

The word "lama" means superior one and strictly speaking it is applicable only to the abbots, but it has now become the general term for all those who come of age in the monastery.

"In the general way," he said, "a child enters the monastery at about the age of seven. A strict examination is made and any defects, physical or mental, will bar his entry."

And Geshi Rimpoche went on to tell me: "The child's horoscope is made out to see what he is suited for and to what department he should be sent. There are many departments of arts and crafts, and each is controlled by an abbot, and those suited to a particular work are sent to that department.

"The budding lama progresses step by step, steeped in all the mythology of their religion, or he may enter one of the colleges if he so desires.

"After many years of preparation, when he reaches the age of twenty-one he asks permission of the Abbot to take part in the services. He is then put through certain initiations, his head is shaved, only a tuft being left on the top. He then presents himself, clad in the garb of a beggar, before the assembled monks in the temple hall and intimates that he accepts the life of a lama freely and of his own choice.

"The abbot then cuts off the remaining tuft of hair and gives him a religious name by which he is henceforth known. His beggar's garb is removed and he is now clothed with the robe of a lama, and a seat is pointed out to him which he afterwards keeps.

"If he chooses later on to follow the inner teachings he is attached to a lama versed in the occult. He must then master

57

metaphysics and the more important subjects allied to the higher teachings.

"He may so advance until no more knowledge is available for him in the monastery and he asks for leave to go and find a master who can give him the knowledge he desires.

Permission is never withheld for such a worthy desire, and he leaves the monastery with only sufficient food and raiment that he can take on his back.

"It is a tremendous task to weather the storm in the Himalayas with no shelter and little food. It is in this trial that he proves his worth. When he finds his teacher no time is lost in beginning his instruction.

"He is told to free his mind from all illusions and shadows of his former life. He is instructed to look into his mind and see what is there. He sees that his mind is filled with selfcreated images which have no power of their own except the power he gives them. He sees that human thought and reactions are largely made up of fear, worry, doubt and ignorance, and he must cast them all aside like he cast aside his beggar's robe.

"He then finds that the Real Self is not composed of thoughts, images or ideas of mind and body and circumstances. He begins to see the falseness of human thinking and this is a vital point in his training.

"Through the cleansing of the mind he develops a one-pointedness in his concentration and direction not known to the outside world.

"He frees himself from all illusion and stands at the door which opens into that which is behind all things, and is no longer a slave to his thoughts, feelings and reactions.

Chapter III

"He is then shown how easy it is to control the functions of the body, the beat of the heart, and the circulation of his blood. His body becomes a keen instrument which responds to his direction, his mind is alert and clear, there is no longer any confusion in it, and it is ready to obey his slightest command. But this is just the beginning of the way, and he must find the rest of the way himself and by himself; for no one can show it to him."

"It was at this stage where you were when you came here, my son," said Geshi Rimpoche.

I thanked him for the clear view he had given me and I now understood. Then he said to me as he put his hand on my shoulder: "You are worthy, my son, of the trust I have put in you, and I will be beside you, with your other august guides you have had all your life. Some you have already spoken to."

I said, "Yes, and you know all about it."

"Oh yes," he affirmed, "I know them all, there is no division between the invisible and the visible. Only man himself has created the division through his ignorance of the Truth of his Being."

After supper we sat and listened to Geshi Rimpoche's favourite pieces. The atmosphere was perfect for the soft flowing parts of Mendelssohn. I needed the harmonising effects, and Geshi Rimpoche knew it. I had seen the conflict within myself dissolve away, yet I could still see conflict external to myself. There was still something left that I had not yet discerned, there was a certain amount of resentment left in me, but I was satisfied that that also would be revealed. I was now aware that my freedom was not yet as complete as I thought it was.

CHAPTER IV

It was early morning when I awoke, and the music of the night before was still part of me. The soft flowing parts of Mendelssohn which Geshi Rimpoche had chosen were still "living" with me, and there was a sense of deeper freedom now.

He also was up early. It was summer-time and he told me that he seldom missed seeing the sun rise in the morning. As yet it had not risen. It was just beginning to show a reflection from the tops of the mountains covered with the eternal snows.

We both sat down to watch the rays of colour changing from dark red into the brighter shades. Nowhere in the world can there be seen a more glorious sight than in Tibet when the sun is rising or when it is setting behind the snowclad peaks of the mighty Himalayas.

As the sun rose, the rays were reflected from the snow that had become crisp and crystal-like through the below-zero atmosphere during the night. All the colours of the rainbow began to show themselves in the dark blue background of the sky, while the sun changed from dark shades of red into the lighter shades of orange; the sky lost its dark blue background, the twinkling stars faded, and the bright blue background of the sky appeared.

I was lost in thought at this wonderful sight. Then Geshi Rimpoche broke the spell.

He said, "You know, music has colours, and if only we could hear the sound of this harmony of colour it would make a perfect symphony---it would be like the music of the spheres."

"Yes," I replied, "the Creator created a reflection of Himself in the great masters of music."

61

Chapter IV

I wanted to draw him out on this subject, and I gave him the lead. He must have read my thoughts, for he said: "My son, I would like to talk to you this morning about music. It is part of your study, you know. I do not mean just the composition of notes but the creative and curative value of music."

"There is nothing I would like better," I assured him.

He closed his eyes, as he always did when speaking of the deeper things of Life, and in that beautiful mellow-toned voice, as if he had himself touched the very source of music, he began: "Beautiful music is but the transposing of the music of the spheres, the expression of the great Divine Intelligence who creates all within Himself, for there cannot be anything outside Him, He being Infinite in nature, even the earth and all that is in it and on it. The soul of the earth reflects the creative expression in light, sound and colour, in rhythmic splendour," and he went on:

"Music is the eternal rhythmic waves of the Infinite expressing Himself throughout His own creation, and mankind is the most perfected instrument for this purpose. Those rhythmic waves of light, sound and colour are always flowing in perfect harmony. Any discordant note does not come from the creative Source but through man's inability to reflect the perfect rhythm."

I felt at the moment that I was in tune with that perfect rhythm and could hear dimly, as if away in the distance, music that was not of this earth. I had touched the hem of the garment of the Master and could hear what he was hearing; indeed, he stopped as if he also was listening to that perfect blending of light, sound and colour that was beyond the mind, for man's mind could reflect it only when in tune with it. Man's mind could not produce it, for it was the Eternal speaking.

Chapter IV

"Yes," he continued, "the song of the birds, the trees in the forest, the rivers, the mountains, all have their own perfect harmonious rhythm. I have often lingered in that harmony and felt that same creative rhythm within myself. In this way I became one with the rhythm of the Universal Forces of Nature and learned to control them because they were part of myself.

"In this way, in the silence of these great mountains, I learned the magic of Nature's Forces---things that few people know---and I could reveal to your scientists knowledge that would lead to greater discoveries of the Universal Forces operating through the atomic structure of which they know very little as yet.

"When I was in tune with this rhythm I could sing with the birds, the wild animals were no longer wild, even the mountains could speak to me, and I could play my favourite instrument, the violin, to keep hundreds spellbound, because I never resisted this flow, no matter what happened about me; it was as if the rhythm was part of me."

Now, I thought to myself, this is news, for I did not know about his violin, and I must ask him to play for me. This I did later, and never had I heard such music. It was music that had not been written, and more perfect melody I had never heard before, or have heard since; it was his own composition.

He paused. He was sensitive to my thoughts; I knew that he knew them, and I smiled.

Then he continued: "Just as thinking comes before asking or acting, so does the music of the spheres come before feeling and playing, and it is this feeling that inspires the expression. The music of the spheres plays upon the soul that is tuned to it. The soul is the harp upon which the Spirit-God within expresses Himself, and according to the fullness of your heart so will His harmony be expressed in and through you. That is why you must learn to love everything, for God is everything. To love God with all your heart is to love your neighbour as yourself. Then He can speak in and through you, and there is nothing impossible unto you; anything you ask, the Universe will be quick to complete it. Above all, you will have harmony in your mind and body."

"The more harmonious you are," he said, "the more receptive you will be; so will your soul and body express Him who ever remains within you, for it is He alone that worketh perfection. Thus you will be strong in mind and body, even though many years have passed; the Ever-present is ever-present, the same always, for there is no ageing of the Spirit of God."

At once I realised how he had kept so young, both in mind and body. He stopped again as if my thoughts were spoken aloud, though I had not uttered a word.

"Yes," he said, "what the inner is, so the outer must be."

Then he continued: "Rhythm and expression are the essential factors in music.

Execution without rhythm has no colour-blending, but harmony and execution vitalised by rhythm are the perfect blending of all the colours, like the colours of the spectrum intermingling one with another in perfect unison. It is this blending of the colours that affects the souls of those who are listening."

Then he added, as if a thought was passing through his mind: "You will hear more about this later on."

I was going to say something, but words would not come, and he continued: "The perfect rhythm is like the ebb and flow of the tide--- nothing can withstand its smooth and regular power. For the Infinite Creativeness is within the perfect rhythm. The Creator and His creation are 'one,' not separate, and *we* are in no way separated from the rhythm of the Divine Intelligence expressing Itself."

"This perfect rhythm," he explained, "is flowing through and over the earth from north to south and is polarised by the sun and the moon, rising in the east and setting in the west.

"This force now becomes electro-magnetic; it keeps the earth on its axis and holds everything on it by the power of its magnetic attraction. Should this electro-magnetic force cease to be, other magnetic currents would draw the earth towards it at such a terrific speed that it would break up into the cosmic dust out of which it arose. In this electro-magnetic force lies the secret of great discoveries."

"The perfect rhythm," he said, "is rejuvenation: it makes the mind alert, the body firm.

That is why we use music in healing; the mind is then freed from distractions which cause tension, and Nature is given an opportunity to harmonise every cell in the body. Mind and body then become electro-magnetic, in perfect harmony."

"The music of the spheres," he continued, "can be said to be the rhythm of the Eternal Heart of God, moving outwards and returning like the bloodstream, circulating to every cell in the body and returning to the heart to be renewed continuously. So does the pulse of the one Life move through every living soul. According to our mental and emotional freedom so is the rhythm expressed."

He added: "If the mechanism is in a state of confusion, so will the rhythm be confused.

Your thoughts and feelings fly through the body cells and then out into the atmosphere and beyond."

Chapter IV

I thought again to myself, "just like a broadcasting station."

"Yes," he said, "the whole of the ether is magnetised with these electro-magnetic waves enabling the whole world to hear and feel the Divine Broadcasting station all at the same time.

East, west, north, south, up into the stratosphere and down into the bowels of the earth, there is nowhere where it is not.

"Here we are on the roof of the world, the hub as you may call it, and with our thought strongly impregnated with the Love of God we can help the world as we tune-in to the rhythm of the Universe which comes from the Heart of God."

I said to myself, "Geshi Rimpoche is not only showing me what music is but also he is revealing to me deeper knowledge, all at the same time."

He must have caught my thought again, for he said: "Practice is necessary so that you can control your instrument, but do not limit yourself to your instrument. I have heard music played badly on a good instrument and have heard beautiful expression from a very indifferent instrument, and this applies to individuals as well---the Love of God is Eternal and Everpresent and no one is separated from it.

"No two people play alike because of the many shades in feeling. While some see the notes on the score, others feel the music in their soul. There is one saving grace for bad music," he said with a touch of humour, "and that is that it does not last. The predominating harmonious rhythm makes it fade away into nothingness whence it arose, because it is not Real. Like an error in a sum, where does it go when the sum is corrected? It fades into nothingness, simply because there is no law upon which it can rest. The law of mathematics, only, exists, likewise the law of harmony."

Chapter IV

"The blending of colour," he explained, "is the secret of harmony. Have you ever seen an inharmonious blending of colour in Nature? No, there is no such thing. So is it with sound, for sound is colour and colour is sound, and Nature is expressing herself in light, colour and sound continuously.

"While practising, you should know what the sound should be. Do not force it; something inside you will tell you when it is right. Make your execution as perfect as possible, then gradually increase the tempo till you play with speed and accuracy, without strain.

Remember, rhythm and expression must not be sacrificed for speed." "There is also such a thing as over-practice," he pointed out, "the fresher you are the better your movements will be. The mind repeats what is done, and therefore a wrong habit is difficult to correct. A rest period is good because it gives the mind time to re-arrange the consciously-made movements. Accuracy is therefore essential. Actually you are learning to play when you are not playing, for the mind takes up the work when you give it the opportunity.

"You have found that after a rest you can play a piece easily, a piece you found difficult before. This is because the mind has been making the adjustments while you rested the mechanism. It is like a problem you try to solve, one which for a time eludes you. You go to sleep and when you awake you have the solution. The mind has worked it out when you gave it the opportunity.

"In making your movements you must hear and feel as well as lose yourself in music.

"Self-consciousness confuses the mechanism. The mind can think of only one thing at a time. Thus when you are thinking of yourself, and then the music, you are moving backwards and forwards, from one to the other.

The easiest way to overcome this habit is to lose yourself in the rhythm. You will soon find that the rhythm takes up the space between the two conscious mental activities, and then the inner mind begins to work with freedom, for it is from there that you really play. Is is all within, and, as you practise, your movements, your music, your rhythm are all merged into one as you play. Be as calm as the depth of the ocean---then you will reflect God's perfect harmony."

"The Eternal looks out through humanity," he went on, "and through humanity He spins the weave and web---the rhythm of Life. Never imitate anybody. You must express your own individuality; then you will have the originality that amounts to genius.

"The blending of the notes is very important. Emphasis should be made at the beginning of the phrase, a little more value should be given to the first note in the bar, and listen carefully to the overtones, blending them into a perfect phrase.

"In legato melodies do not cut off a note with a hard edge before the next one comes in; listen to the overtones, and let the timbre or quality sound until such time as it reaches the point where the progression must go on. Then smoothly flow into the next note without a break, so that you cannot tell where one ends and the other begins. The perfect blending of the overtone carries the body of the music in harmonious rhythm."

"I thought to myself, here is something rare put into words; I almost felt the smooth flowing tones within myself. I have studied music for some years, first with the violin, then with the bagpipes. I must have been fairly good for I happened to win the championship at Stamfordbridge at the Coronation Highland Gathering in 1911, and I knew what Geshi Rimpoche said was true. As he spoke, his voice like music; he might have been playing a piece of exquisite beauty.

Chapter IV

Then he continued: "Watch the progression and shape of your phrase so that you can move naturally to the point of climax, and then fall back again into the next phrase, with ease and smoothness; this gives a sense of rhythm that you seldom hear, unless it is from a great artist."

Here he opened his eyes and said, "Would you like me to go on?"

Until then I had not spoken and I at once replied: "Oh, yes, please, this is what I have been waiting for, ever since I began to study music."

There had been a certain amount of tension in my concentration because I had not wanted to miss a word, and I think he knew it.

"All right," he responded, "we will go on," and he proceeded:

"The point of climax may be treated in different ways according to the inner feeling and interpretation.

"For instance, in an appassionata passage you may gradually accelerate tempo and strengthen tone, giving more stress to each succeeding emphasis up to the point of climax, or you may broaden successive chords, holding back the final accent for a breathless moment to increase intensity.

"A device used by Beethoven is to pile up a chord passage, strength upon strength, with increasing accent, but the expected crash on the final emphasis does not eventuate. Instead, we get a chord played suddenly pianissimo, surprising the ear with unexpected beauty and the realisation of a depth of inner mystery.

"Mozart, when asked what he thought the most effective device in music, said, 'No music.'

Chapter IV

"Used with artistry the complete silence of a pause in music, or the moment of poise at the height of a phrase, can be fraught with the greater sense of inner meaning and beauty.

"You may move your audience on the wings of a soaring phrase, then hold them suspended at the height, revealing in a moment of time the Eternity of Spirit, then drop back on the descent of the phrase to the light of common day."

I drew a deep breath, for here was a treat that music lovers would deeply enjoy; even those who had risen to the peak of their artistry could benefit from it. By the time this thought pass through my mind Geshi Rimpoche was proceeding and I had to pull myself together so as not to miss a word. I am happily blessed with a sort of photographic mind for things that interest me, and these impressions seem to be indelible. I was fortunate, too, in having made a few notes to remind me of various points.

He paused and then resumed: "Or you may move through a legato melody and, with a slight hesitation, lingeringly delay the moment of beauty, increasing the anticipation so that when the sound strikes the ear it comes with exquisite relief, satisfying the longed-for fulfillment of beauty."

"Again," he said, "you may reach the point of climax and linger on it lovingly with a caressing touch, but this freedom must be obtained within the law---that is, the realisation of the rhythmic flow---the balance of one phrase with the other and the co-ordination of the whole into perfect unity. It is like the perfect union between two souls in the bliss of a perfect love, two souls that become one in that complete and final ecstasy.

"Chopin had a wonderful airy grace with which his fingers glided, almost flew, over the keyboard, producing a tone like velvet, a slightly veiled yet silvery sonorousness. Qualities which Chopin regarded as paramount were delicacy of touch, intelligence of conception, purity of feeling. To Chopin the worst sin was a dull mechanical dexterity."

Geshi Rimpoche waited for a moment as if to let the last few words sink in, and then he continued: "Throughout the whole of his playing Chopin employed a certain rocking movement with a most enchanting effect, the undulation of the melody being like a skiff upon the bosom of the tossing waves. This peculiar style of execution was his idiosyncrasy, his sign manual so to speak. It set the seal upon all his compositions in which it is indicated by the term *tempo rubato*. This apparent disregard for time was with him a charming originality of manner, a flexible fluctuating languorous movement, a measured rhythm balance and sway best comprehended by his own countrymen who, having an innate, intuitive understanding of his meaning, were able to follow the fluctuation of the aerial and spiritual blue which it represented."

Stopping for a moment to think, Geshi Rimpoche said: "I am sure I read something like that about Chopin---I think it was Moschiles who wrote it," and he continued: "Purity of expression can result only when you are true to yourself, that is, when you express your own inner depth according to the clarity of your thought, interpretation and execution. So will your hearers receive the message and meaning which you wish to convey, and this message and meaning will correspond to the degree in which you open yourself to the flow of the Infinite Intelligence---the degree in which you realise that there is no separation in the one Life that binds us all together."

I felt like saying, as Schuman said, "that in the playing of an instrument, you must be one with it, and he who cannot play 'with' it cannot play at all."

Chapter IV

"The reason for many failures with those of great promise," Geshi Rimpoche added, "is that they do not know that the Creator and His creation are one, not separate. It makes all thedifference when this is understood, not merely as an idea, by experiencing the fact that Spirit alone has voice, that God expresses Himself through the voice, through harmony, through light, sound, colour and form. He is harmony, love, wisdom, power. In this lies the power of God in man, for God *is* man, 'I and the Father are one.' "The word was with God, and God was that word, and that word was made flesh,' but the flesh had no say in the matter, so the word remains immortal. We are *not* born of the blood or the will of the flesh, nor of the will of man, but of God."

He looked at me as if to see that I thoroughly understood what he had said which I was thankful to feel that I had done.

"Those who would express themselves in music," he affirmed, "should remember that God made the perfect instrument for His own self-expression. 'Be ye perfect as your Father in Heaven is perfect.' The soul receives, and the mind and brain direct the mechanism. If in your mind you have an idea that the mechanism is defective, that thought tends to express itself, and the more you try to get pefect expression the more active will be the reverse thought. This is what induces many failures. Remember it is continuous practice with rest periods for assimilation, with conscious awareness of the perfect rhythm, that makes a genius. One must practise slowly to master the execution of the composition. Do not slur over a difficult part; take it slowly at first and increase the tempo, but with accuracy. Know that you were born with dominion over all things.

"Understand the impersonal unity in all things, disregard personal separation, live in the conscious realisation of your oneness with the Creator of all mankind. Love your neighbour as yourself.

Chapter IV

"Play and sing with your heart full of love, let it be a harp of exquisite melody and beauty --- and those in Heaven above will rejoice as they feel your oneness with them."

I was spellbound by his understanding, his wisdom, his knowledge of all the important things in Life. I sat there deep in thought, and then I heard his voice saying in a different tone, almost as if it were a command, "Arise my son, we must go now, for there is a lot for you to do in the time you are with us and you must be on your way."

"Yes," I said, "but I would like to remain with you a little longer."

"That will be arranged later," he replied. "In the mean time others are waiting to see you in the flesh. It is already known among the Tibetan Yogi and Masters in the Ok Valley that you are on your way, but I would like you first to go along the Ha Chu Valley as far as Ha Dzong. There are eight monasteries quite close together on the way.

"Here is a letter to Dar Tsang, head of the Yangtang Monastery; he will put you in touch with the others. He is a master of Tumo. I have made all arrangements for you to see and understand this Science."

"Yes," I said, "I have heard of this Science, the control of the elements, of heat and cold."

"Yes, it is interesting, but after all it does not reveal Reality, though I would like you to see it done, and perhaps, you will get a few lessons in it," and he smiled.

"In the monastery of Gonsaka," he continued, "you will learn the art of travelling over vast spaces in a very short time. This is done by a form of levitation in trance. You will also see, in the Takohu

Monastery, the practice of mental telepathy. This subject is very interesting and I want you to pay particular attention to it because it will be of great value to you later on."

(This I did indeed find valuable, for, when I was in many different lands, although I could not speak the language, yet I could read the mind.)

"This will take you a month or more of your time."

I inquired: "What about my friend, doe he come with me?"

"No," he replied, "he will be waiting for you in the Ok Valley when you arrive there."

The following day I read all the instructions that were to help me on my way, and I duly set out after taking leave of Geshi Rimpoche and my friend. With me I took my bearer, my interpreter, my bodyguard, our ponies, and one mule, leaving the others at Lingmatang, as I would have to come back that way. I was not going in the opposite direction, away from the trade route to Lhasa. I was going now behind the Himalayas that separated Bhutan from Tibet.

I was told that the track was merely a footpath, very dangerous in parts because of the many landsides.

Snow leopards also were in this district. These animals look like a cross between a tiger and a wolf. They prey on the mountain goats, and are very fleet and sure of foot. They have been known to attack travellers on the path at dangerous points. On the way we saw a couple of them but they were well out of our reach. The nomads--- the people who live in the plains ---keep a large number of mastiff dogs to protect their stock from marauders.

We crossed the fast-flowing river, the Ama Chu, at a place called Geling Market, a market place where the inhabitants exchange things. Very little money is used; the people barter goods and seem to do very well. The exchange seems to even itself out, I was told. We passed through the market place and made our way down to a place called Sharithang at the lower end of the Chumbi Valley.

Yatung is situated about the middle of the Chumbi Valley (of which I spoke in a previous chapter). To get to Lhasa you turn to the left, but we turned to the right. The Chumbi Valley at this time of the year, May and June, is prolific with wild flowers. The mountainsides right down to the edge of the valley were covered with rhododendron trees in full bloom. The different colours, red, pink, white and purple made a wonderful picture. Where the rhododentron trees reached the valley floor where were large Chinese poppies, each at least five inches in diameter, and the stems were about five feet tall. The petals were a rich yellow shade with pink edges, really beautiful to look at.

I said to my interpreter: "In London these would be worth a fortune, and here they are growing prolifically and nobody wants them."

The floor of the valley was covered with wild aconite, wild gentian and delphinium.

Here was a plant which is used extensively in *materia medica*, especially for all types of inflammation, and it is considered the most useful drug in homeopathy ---the famous aconitum.

Gentian, a good tonic and an excellent stomachic, was also here. In this far inaccessible land these plants could be had by the cart load.

As we passed out of the valley we came upon the most rugged and dangerous path I had yet seen. It was not more than about two feet wide in some place, and ran along the edge of a steep precipice with a sheer drop of over a thousand feet into the Ha Chu River below. I made me dizzy to look down. In one place we passed under a rock jutting right over the path; it would be several thousand tons in weight. I walked under it, backward and forward, several times, just to experience the thrill of it.

I thought that a mountainslide might happen, for the rock hung well over the precipice.

But it held on to the mountain, and how it did so was a mystery to me. Perhaps one day it will hurl itself down a thousand feet into the river bed below; if so, it will make a roaring, crashing noise like thunder.

We climbed and climbed until we reached the top of the pass and could pick out, in the distance, the valley of Wong Chu. In the foreground we could see Ha Dzong, and dotted here and there on the side of the mountain were the monasteries.

It was a new experience for me to see so many large monasteries so near one another, perched on the mountain side.

Going down the pass was even more strenuous than ascending. The bottom of the pass opened into the valley of Wong Chu, through which the Ha Chu River flowed. There we were met by a number of Tibetans on shaggy ponies.

I said to my bodyguard: "These fellows look like bandits!"

"Yes," he said, "they are."

We were outnumbered by about five to one. They closed slowly around us expecting us to put up a fight, but I knew this would be suicidal, and within me I felt that there would be some means to overcome our difficulties.

Chapter IV

These brigands think that banditry is a gentleman's occupation, and they disdain any other kind of "work." They began to go through our possessions, and I could see that they meant to take all we had, including our ponies. All this would place us in a very awkward predicament, and I was almost at my wit's end what to do. Then suddenly I thought of my artificial eye. I knew these fellows were very superstitious, and I had already learned something about their religion.

One of their most feared gods was a white god with only one eye, a god who brought havoc, even death, upon those who angered him. Therefore these fellows regularly propitiate him with gifts of all kinds to sooth his wrath. So, knowing this, I went straight in among them and made some weird noises calling in Tibetan for the seven hells to open up under them. I took out my artificial eye, showed it all round, and then put it back again. You should have seen their faces! Their eyes opened wide, and in fear and trembling they threw down our things, got on their ponies and fled---we could hardly see them for dust. We split our sides laughing when we realised what an artificial eye could do. They gave us wide berth after this, and we never saw them again. But we happened to hear weird stories about the white god who had dropped over the mountain into the Wong Chu Valley. They had taken me to be the angry god whom they feared so much. I never let the secret leak out, that an artificial eye did the trick.

What added colour to the story of the mysterious visitor was that a young lad, about nineteen years old, had the misfortune to fall down the mountainside and dislocate his shoulder. I happened to come along and set it for him. The shoulder had been "out" for only half an hour and was easily put right. This incident meant additional fame for the "white god" and I heard all about it when I got back to Lingmatang, for Geshi Rimpoche greeted me with: "My son, your fame is greater than mine, and you have been in the country for only such a little while."

Chapter IV

We laughed heartily, you may be sure, about it all.

CHAPTER V

After we crossed the Kyu La Pass, which is nearly 16,000 feet above sea level, and after all the excitement we had with our gentlemen friends, the bandits at the foot of the pass, it was rather late when we reached the rest hut at a place called Damtang, 11,000 feet above sea level.

The floor of Tibet averages between 10,000 and 12,000 feet above sea level, with towering snowclad mountains on all sides, accessible only over passes 15,000 to 20,000 feet high, many of them impassable in winter. Tibet covers and area of over 600,000 square miles in which about two million people live. Some of these merely exist, but others are relatively wealthy. The contrast is very evident.

Although it was late in the evening it was still daylight. The sun was setting over the mountains behind Tenchen Monastery which lay hidden in the mountainside, about five miles away. I decided that we would remain in the hut for the night and get to Yangtang about ten o'clock next morning; so my bearer got out the cooking utensils, lit a fire, and cooked a satisfying meal of roast chicken and roast potatoes. We had come a long way and eaten very little that day, and naturally I was hungry, and ate with relish; it seemed to me the best meal I ever had.

My bearer happened to be clever with his accordion and I got him to play some of his own songs. These sounded romantic and fitted in with the surroundings.

Where the hut was situated there was a deep gorge to the front and a mountain at the back. This produced a distinct echo, more distinct than I have heard anywhere in the world. It sounded as if two people were playing at the same time, one away in the distance. The chanting melodies seemed to dovetail into each other as if one was answering the other. It was well after 11 p.m. before we went to bed. I was tired and slept like a log.

In the morning when I awoke the sun was just rising. I never miss the rising sun or its setting if I can help it. On this occasion the sunrise seemed to do something to me. The wonderful panorama of colouring awakened in me the inner mysterious feeling which Tibet held for me, for Tibet is shrouded in mystery: the most superstitious and the most sublime are side by side. Indeed, Tibet is a land of extremes, with the darkest ignorance and the greatest wisdom, where miracles seem as easy as breathing. There is the wildest of the wild--the rugged in Nature, and the most beautiful, the mountains and the valleys. There are the great and the small, the storms and the calm, the heat of the day and the cold of the night. These follow one another; as one moves in, the other moves out, almost at the same time. There is the filthiest and the most meticulous, the worst and the finest, in human character. It is truly a country of contrasts.

As these thoughts pass through my mind the sun's rays were striking the portals of Tenchen monastery. I could hear, in the distance, the *chonghas* booming out their long deep tones and the booming of the great gongs while the lamas' deep voices chanted *Om Mani Padme Hum.*

As I looked down the valley the shadows of the mountains were disappearing. It was a strange feeling that I had, a feeling of sheer wonderment. The air was crisp with cold of the night and the wind was coming our way wafting the scent of incense. This gave further enchantment to the scene---the sun rising over the mountains, the rushing river threading through the valley, the glittering spray reflecting colours like a rainbow, the weird music, the lamas' deep voices and the incense, these things alone were worth coming for.

Some monasteries have great incense jars which stand above the portals of the monastery facing the valley, in which incense is kept

Chapter V

continually burning. As the sun rose, the whole atmosphere gave me that feeling which comes to one in anticipation of the revelation of some mysterious force hidden for thousands of years.

Three monasteries were within a few miles of each other, Tenchen, Gyamdu and Yangtang. I knew that Yangtang was the furthest of the three and was the monastery of the yellow sect which I had to contact first.

We moved down the path that led down the side of the rushing river and the spray was blown on our faces by the wind that was now forced up the valley, the mountains creating a funnel through which the wind blew forcibly, causing even the stones on the path to be flickered in our faces.

We came to a flimsy bridge held together by bamboo rope, and, as I stepped on it, it swayed from side to side. It was suspended from both sides of the river, where the water rushed between two great rocks, forming a deep gorge. One snap of the bamboo rope and I would be no more, for nothing could live in that great torrent of glacier water with its bluewhite foam lashing against the sides of the rocks as it rushed through.

We got to the other side and made our way up a steep grade for about two miles to the monastery of Yangtang.

It must have been a strange sight to the lamas to see us coming up the steep steps that had been hewn out of the rock upon which the monastery stood, for nothing like it had happened before. I felt a little queer, for I did not have my friend with me to speak to me, and I had to introduce myself with the letter Geshi Rimpoche had given me.

When we reached the monastery my interpreter spoke for me. He told the lama who came to meet us that I had a letter from Geshi

Rimpoche to Geshi Dar Tsang. I had already learned patience, as nothing moves quickly in this isolated land of mystery, and in the meantime I obtained permission to look round the monastery.

The conducting lama was an old man with a very intelligent face. I can well remember the look he gave me---it was one of deep wonderment. I could imagine what his thoughts were, such as "What do you want here?" "Where have you come from?" "What sort of a world do you live in?" "What is in that letter from Geshi Rimpoche?"

The walls of Yangtang Monastery were built of great boulders roughly hewn. The total weight of the massive building was impossible to estimate. The walls were about seven feet in thickness, and the great boulders were put together with great skill. How it all had been done was a mystery to me.

The roof was covered with slate about two inches thick, coloured yellow, this being one of the yellow sect monasteries. The way the roof and walls are coloured, I was told, was by making great quantities of coloured wash and pouring it over the roof; the walls were treated in the same way, but in a white wash.

I entered on the ground floor through a great central hall. Around on all sides were the store-rooms. Around the sides above the store-rooms were small chapels used as shrines for the deities. In these shrines were many images of gold and silver, their value beyond estimation.

Above the main temple hall were the various rooms containing the monastic paraphernalia, and surrounding the great main building were other buildings, the living quarters of the lamas.

The main hall door was of immense size, like that of Lingmatang, draped on the sides with massive curtains of rich brocade tasselled with gold. Around the main hall were murals of exquisite beauty. These were the guardian deities and demons of the locality. On the left side was the wheel of Life, and on both sides were large prayer-wheels filled with countless numbers of prayers, mostly with the formula *Om Mani Padme Hum.* The prayer wheels were about eight to ten feet in height and about five to six feet in diameter.

They are turned with a crank handle and each time it revolves a bell rings. This is a sign that your sins have been forgiven. Around the walls of the temple were smaller prayer-wheels, and, as a lama passed one, he gave it a turn with his hand. This by the way, is the means by which he builds up his virture!

I saw numbers of images in gold, studded with precious jewels, probably worth thousands of pounds, and many silken banners, some of them priceless.

The temple had galleries all around, the ceiling was supported by mighty wooden pillars almost twice the thickness of my body, and long silken streamers of rare design hung around them. These are all worked by the lamas, depicting their Buddhas and saints as well as deities who guarded the monastery.

At the far end of the temple hall was the altar and at the foot were hundreds of butter lamps in gold and silver. These were burning and the lama present was refilling them with yak butter (they must be kept burning continuously). On the top of the throne of the altar, which is used only by the Dalai Lama, was suspended a beautiful silken brocade canopy. On the right side was a seat lower, this being the seat of the director of ceremonies, and on the left were similar ones where the abbots sat. The director of ceremonies directs the service and the abbots instruct the lamas.

Chapter V

In front of this were other seats for the high lamas, and then came many long rows of seats about six inches off the floor, all facing one way, up and down the hall (not across as we have them). Each lama sat in Buddha fashion behind one another. A service was in progress, and there were intervals during which tea was served by the tea distributors, each lama carrying his own teacup.

Tea is drunk at all hours, all day, I was told. The tea was brought from the black dingy kitchens where there were large iron pots, some about five feet high and four feet in diameter, into which are put a brick of Chinese tea, a large chunk of rancid butter and a quantity of salt.

This is kept simmering day and night, and water and other ingredients are added when required.

I was told that several million pounds weight of tea are imported each year into Tibet.

The average cups consumed each day by one person amounts to between twenty and thirty cups. Tea seemed to be served all the time the service was going on.

In the centre of the hall were the *chonghas* and gongs. The *chonghas* were about ten feet or more in length, and the large gongs were about five to six feet in diameter. The *chonghas* were supported on stands covered with gold plating, and the gongs were supported on two pillar stands similarly plated.

The *chonghas* were blown in such a way that one set of lamas would "take up" before the other set finished, with the result that a continuous booming note was heard, and at intervals the gongs were struck sounding a deep boom through the whole of the temple. This happened when the lamas reached the *Om* and the *Hum* of *Om Mani Padme Hum.* Inter mingling with this were hundreds of tiny bells tinkling at intervals. All this seemed to be directed by the director of ceremonies.

My letter had at last reached Geshi Dar Tsang, for, during the time that I was so deeply interested in what was going on in the Temple Hall, a lama came to escort me to Geshi Dar Tsang's private quarters.

I was surprised to see a very young-looking man. He spoke to me in Hindustani, which I knew well. His knowledge of Hindustani was extremely good and we got on excellently, and I was glad that I could speak without the use of an interpreter.

He was glad to see me; I took it that he was pleased with Geshi Rimpoche's letter. I did not know what Rimpoche said, not even to-day, for it was written in Tibetan, but it must have carried something very pleasing about me, otherwise I would have received the cold shoulder which is meted out to anyone who tries to visit the sanctum of the most high.

I asked him how he had learned Hindustani and he told me that the Yogi who taught him was an Indian Yogi. I was interested to hear this, for I had been with the Indian Yogi myself.

I said: "I see many much older lamas than you in the monastery; how is it that you, being so young, are at the head of this great monastery?"

He replied: "I am older than any of them, though I do not look it."

Then I asked: "With your knowledge and experience, you do not believe in all this deity and hell business, do you?

"Oh no," he replied, "but all these people have been brought up to know nothing else.

My students who have mastered the art of Tumo know that ritual and superstition are merely to impress the mind, but as you know, I could not teach that to everyone---my life would not be worth living. In fact, I would not be allowed to live! That is what religion is like in this country.

We are at present where the West was at the time of the Spanish Inquisition."

I was surprised that he knew about the brutality of the priesthood. I said: "Perhaps if it was not for the law we might still have persecution? A great many people now have far outdistanced the religious bigots we have even to-day; that is why our churches are mostly empty."

"Mankind," I went on, "is divided by religion, by nationality, by groups, by beliefs, by ideas, only because man will not see how false they are. Once he sees how false these things are he will drop them; then, and then only, will he realise that we are all one. Then man will free himself through the Truth of the One Life in each being, which is the only Real and the only Truth that will set him free."

"You have put it into a nutshell," he said, and he continued: "Ideas are presented to the conscious mind and are received and passed on to the unconscious. Immediately they are accepted or rejected according to the ruling belief or idea held. This is not understanding it is ignorance, but few will see it, because a belief or an idea is a reality to them. They have not yet come to know what an idea is, or how it is formed in the mind by environment, by imitation.

So we have confusion and antagonism in the world which leads to war and misery."

Chapter V

"I agree with you," I said, "I have seen leaders, religious and otherwise, make statements which the unthinking masses accept. So they wave flags and shout. This is the ignorant mob, people who are not capable of examining what is said and it is happening everywhere. Leaders steeped in religious bigotry and extreme nationalism are the curse of our civilisation. It is these people that should be put out of harm's way, for they are the cause of much suffering to unenlightened humanity."

"That is very true," he said, "but the worst of all is that people pray to a God of Love while they are steeped in hatred. Their prayers are idolatrous. Only when they understand how hatred has arisen will they know how to pray to a God of Love.

"Those who live in separation pray to a false god of their own making who hears them *not*. Is this not the teaching of the false prophets we have in our midst all over the world? Each separate religious group claims its religion to be the only true one, and blazons forth the dire penalties that will happen to those who do not accept; hence man is kept in ignorance and is confused and fearful through superstition."

I had found another friend and we made good progress together.

"I think it would be advisable for you to wear the robe of a teacher while you are here." he said, and he handed me a purple robe which I put on. "Geshi Rimpoche tells me in his letter that you are a master of *prana yama* and master of the healing arts."

I said that I had done much healing all over the world and I had been more than successful, but I attributed that to a power that is beyond myself.

"Yes," he concurred, "only when we know that we are nothing then does the Spirit, which is all, manifest in and through us."

Chapter V

He took down a book with notes in his own handwriting in Tibetan, and he turned over the pages till he came to the words he had written there. "He who seeks to save his life will lose it, but he who gives up his life for My sake will retain it."

"In this book," he said, "I have all the sayings of the great Masters, and these sayings I have found to be true."

Then he suddenly changed the subject. "You have come here to know something about Tumo, the control of the elements, of heat and cold. You have allowed yourself a very short time for this. It is one of the more difficult occult Sciences, because the sense of feeling comes into it so much."

"Yes," I said, "I know my time is limited, but I do not want to be really master of the Science of Tumo as long as I can understand it, and by practice I may be able to become at least adaptable."

"Then," he said, "there is no time like the present, so let us begin."

He took me into his inner sanctuary where we sat on very comfortable cushioned stools.

"Then," he began in the tone of the master, "it is not merely an idea to you that Life alone lives, that the body does not live apart from Life. Life alone has consciousness, and the only consciousness the body has is the Life that permeates it by the means of the nervous and vaso systems."

I was amazed at his thorough knowledge of the human frame and told him so. He replied: "The practice of Tumo demands this," and he went on: "Every form arises out of invisible matter, which is the basis of all forms; there is no form separated from it. Now we know that invisible matter can be condensed into a solid mass by a change in consciousness in regard to it. So can solid matter be dissolved into invisible matter by the same process in reverse, but the trouble with most people is that their consciousness is not trained, and feeling interferes with its direction."

I listened very carefully to what he said. "You know well enough," he continued, "in your healing work that feeling and fear that hinder the healing process in the patient."

I replied: "I know that only too well, and it requires a change in consciousness to get beyond it."

"Right," he said, "So when considering the cause and cure of any disease, whether it be of mind or body, we must bear in mind or body, we must bear in mind that matter is plastic to our thoughts and feelings and this is even more important to you in the practice of Tumo. By completely understanding the mental process you will be able to dissolve any condition that is the result of error."

"That is so," I said. "Well," he continued, "heat and cold do not exist in Reality; these 'conditions' exist only in the mind. Spirit, which is the basis of all things, is not affected by heat or cold. When you bring heat and cold together both disappear."

"I understand that," I said.

"Well," he went on, "this is done by breathing exercises with the use of the sound vibrations of the 'Aum' so that it vibrates through the whole of your body. You pass into a subjective state wherein you control the elements; therefore the elements of heat and cold are controlled as well."

I said: "I am beginning to see daylight now."

"Yes, but that is not all. By the constant repetition of the sound of Creation 'Aum' the subjective consciousness becomes aware of the power of both creation and disintegration because they are one, and not separate principles. The sound 'Aum' can be heard in all creation and every form in mineral, vegetable, animal and human spheres. This is the basic sound; the only difference is the difference in vibration."

"Now," he added, "the ether wave and the sound wave mingle together because you sound the 'Aum' while you are aware that the creative force is in your consciousness; then your thought becomes electro-magnetic, which is the controlling factor in both invisible and visible matter. The sound wave is the wave of ponderable matter; therefore you can play with it up and down the scale, from the invisible to the visible---there is no division between them, it is only apparent. Creative thought being in the Consciousness is sending forth into the ether the invisible waves while the sound reduces them to the visible, and here you have what is called materialisation. You comprehend that, don't you?"

"Yes," I answered, "and I know also that those who chant rituals know little of what they are doing. I also know," I said, "that the therapeutic power of sound in harmonious vibrations exercises an influence on the mind and body, for one is but the product of the other."

"It is the colour of the sound that creates the effect," he said. "Colour affects the ethereal and astral sheaths that penetrate the body, and if the 'Aum' is sounded with understanding and accuracy while the breath of Life is performed it will harmonise all the cells of the body and keep you young. When this is generally known a great civilisation will arise."

"It will be seen," he said, "that the only power comes from the Spirit which is Whole and is everywhere and everpresent, and is the source of all things including man. For 'Now' is eternity; there is no such thing as *time* in the everpresent. The past and the future do not exist outside man's mind."

Chapter V

"Now," he said, "breathe as I direct and sound the 'Aum' as you let the breath out. The sound must be your own tone, which is on the Key A."

So I began to breathe as he directed. (This I cannot give here because of the danger to the uninitiated). A semi trance state was indeed induced.

"Now, again sound the 'Aum' as you breathe out---the sound flowing from head to foot; and as you feel its vibration send a current of Life, by being conscious of It, through your body, and you will feel that your body is on fire. The feeling of the heat helps you. Now, do you understand?"

"Yes, I do" I said, for I felt as if my body was on fire, and I added, "Now I can see that the basis is feeling."

After several practices I was given the opportunity of doing the real thing.

One morning we started climbing the mountain, reaching the snow line at about 9 p.m. (we had climbed nearly all day). When the sun went down it began to freeze several points below zero. I sat between two of his pupils who were proficient in the Science of Tumo. I started the practice as I was instructed. The heat was terrific and the snow began to melt around me, running away in rivulets.

I asked if this was caused by my own efforts or by those on each side of me. He said: "You did exceptionally well; I put the others on each side only to help you."

I was quite pleased with the result, but I knew that it would take years of practice to be a master of Tumo.

I wanted to know how it was done, and I was satisfied. I continued the practice for another ten days till the usual great yearly ceremony at the monastery took place. Then I saw what could really be done with the elements of heat and cold.

Dar Tsang and two of his best pupils took out of a blazing fire white hot bars of iron and put them in their mouths. I could hear the sizzling that came from the moisture in their mouths. They bent these pieces of white hot iron into loops while still in their mouths. There was not a mark or a burn to be seen. I could not go near these bars of iron, so fierce was the heat.

Crowds of lamas from other monasteries, people from all the villages around, came to see the parades and the religious dances of the lamas.

Later, Geshi Dar Tsang took a thick piece of solid steel and turned it into a knot. He did this by means of dematerialization. The material became pliable in his hands, and like a piece of wire he turned it into a knot and tied it.

When I took this knotted steel in my hands, with all my strength I could not even move it.

Shortly afterwards Dar Tsang took it again and untied the knot and made the steel rod straight again. Yes, it was hard to believe.

I knew it took years to perform such feats; even after years of practice few succeed. But the fact that I saw it done with my own eyes convinced me that the seemingly impossible was possible.

Jesus was a great Master and did things far greater than we know of. But the same power that existed then, exists now and will continue to exist because It is Eternal and Everpresent. If we can only get rid of the idea of the solidity of matter and the idea of our own impotence, we could work wonders. Jesus knew this, otherwise he would not have said: "These things I do, greater things shall you do if ye will but understand." He also said faith would move mountains.

But your faith must not be like that of the person who had a knoll in front of her house which hid the view of the sea. When she said, "If ye have sufficient faith ye can say to this mountain, Be buried in the sea and it sahll be done," she went to her window, looked at the knoll and said, "Ye shall be buried in the sea." When she got up the next morning she went to the window and saw that the knoll was still there. She exclaimed, "I knew it would be there all the time."

Wonders have been done in healing all over the world through what we call "Faith."

Thousands of so-called incurable cases have been healed through the agency of Faith. The many miraculous cures attributed to me alone run into many hundreds, but this I know, "I of my own self am nothing, it is the Spirit of the Father within than does the work," the same Life being in the healer and the one being healed.

This, however, must not be a mere platitude but a living experience at the moment, beyond time, beyond ideas, beyond mind. For what is in the mind is but an idea of It, or a belief in It, but that is not It. The word "God" is not God, what you make up in your mind about God is not God, and only when you see the falseness of words, ideas, beliefs, that are hinding the Real, will the Real manifest.

Then the Livingness that is not of time is renewed in your every moment of time.

To try to recapture the moment that is past is useless, because the moment that is past has become a memory which is not the "Living Now." The "Now" is a Livingness that is Eternal and you

cannot make an image of It because you do not know what It is---
you only know that It is.

To imagine it will come again is like "to-morrow," which never
comes: it is always tomorrow.

Trying to become is seeking something that is ever-present and
therefore you can never realise it. Only by living It, can It be
experienced.

Being it Now! Living moment to moment in the Ever-present,
and experiencing It every moment through the expression of Love
and Affection, which is *Reality.* At that moment there is no right or
wrong, no past of future, only the Eternal "Now."

"The Father and I are One." Therefore the self that stands in the
way must be dissolved before the Real comes into being.

"I am the Life, and Life is Love and Love is Reality."

To love your neighbour as yourself you must love your Real Self
that is in your neighbour because there is no division in Reality.

CHAPTER VI

At the Festival of Yangtang Monastery I met Geshi Malapa of the Gonsaka Monastery and Geshi Tung La of the Takohu Monastery, both charming fellows and well versed in their respective sciences. They could also speak Hindustani, which seemed to be their second language. I was glad, because I could carry on a conversation necessary to understand their instructions to me on each of their respective sciences.

I pursuaded Geshi Dar Tsang to come with me. He was pleased that I asked him, for he wanted to see the progress of both Geshi Malapa's and Geshi Tung La's chelas. There was a strong bond among the three of them, and they had a companionable contest to see whose chelas had made the most progress.

So the next day we made our way to Gonsaka. I was given one of the abbot's rooms.

He was at Ganden Monastery, going through a revised course in medicine. This course, I was told, included physiology, physics, botany, and science of the mind. It is in no way comparable with our Western curriculum, being much more crude in some ways, yet much more advanced in others.

Geshi Malapa said that he took his name from the great saint Malarepa who lived to a great age and composed over 100,000 verses revealing his secret knowledge. Malarepa was known as the great miracle worker. His best known feat was to fly to the summit of Mount Kailas by means of levitation in order to demonstrate to the people there that the faith and knowledge he possessed were greater than that of the Bon priests who failed to accomplish such a feat. Hence schools and colleges were formed for the purpose of studying and developing these miraculous powers, and for many years lamas taught by him developed great powers and were credited with mighty miracles. Malapa said that the Gonsaka

Monastery was once one of these colleges but was now turned into a monastery, "hence I took on the name Malapa, a abbreviation of Malarepa."

It was Malarepa's powers that sustained him when he was cut off by the deep snows and glaciers of Mount Everest during the winter.

"First of all," said Malapa, "my pupils must learn levitation through the practice of special breathing excercises. The body then becomes light; sometimes bodies become so light that they have to be weighed down to prevent their floating away."

I said that I had seen levitation in India but he laughed and declared that was child's play.

"First of all," he said, "I take a raw boy lama over fourteen years but under eighteen years, because the power of the lung-gom-pa is obtained only after a long course of probationary exercises. The breathing must be carefully regulated; the devotee must have perfect control of his mind and body. The body must be completely motionless, also there must be the ability to sink into a deep trance which enables him to use inner forces, thereby reversing the polarity at will.

I said: "I understand from Yoga that, as the free energy in the atmosphere is pumped into the body through certain breathing exercises, the body becomes light, so that at will it can e moved in any direction at speed, medium or slow, according to the desired effect required."

"Yes," he affirmed, "the flying lama, or what we call the lung-gom-pa, is an astounding person. He goes into a trance, and some people believe that the body is inhabited by a spirit, but that is not so.

Chapter VI

"After a long period of exercises, gravitation is overcome because the air, being lighter, saturates the body and makes it buoyant, and then the polarity is reversed. By this means the lung-gom-pa moves at great speed over long distances, over mountains and valleys, without fatigue. Fatigue is brought about by the force of gravity when one has to make an effort to move the body because it is attracted to the earth.

"The lung-gom-pa takes a direct line to his destination, and the speed up the mountains and across the valleys is not altered. He goes up the mountain as fast as he goes along the plains, and more than one hundred miles can be covered in a day, and one lung-gom-pa whom I know can cover even a greater distance.

"The fact that there are few of us is borne out by the fact that it takes a long time to accomplish the art---many try but few succeed---because it is perhaps the most difficult of all the occult Sciences."

I remarked that it would be most interesting to witness this marvellous feat.

He said: "You are more than fortunate to witness it, and it is because Geshi Rimpoche, whom we reverence, asked that you should be given the opportunity."

I said: "I have no intention of trying to master this Science, for I have not the time---you see, my work is healing, but the privilege that I may know how it is done, and am allowed to see it, will help me in my own work."

"Then in the morning we will go to our practice ground, which is guarded while we exercise, and there you will be able to witness the lung-gom-pa."

So the next morning we went down to the secluded valley which was behind another range of smaller mountains, where there was a long flat area. Geshi Malapa had only three chelas. He said that three were enough to teach in one life-time.

I watched the three chelas being instructed how to breathe. They had been practising for the last ten years Malapa told me.

Three mounds of earth were built up into cones, and the chelas would sit crossedlegged in Buddha fashion. Gradually they would rise off the ground, reach above the coneshaped mound, and gradually come down upon the top. This was done several times, and then they stood on their feet---this was the most difficult part. Gradually they rose off the ground, one foot placed over the other; and by a series of rhythmic bounds, their eyes gazing into the distance, they moved as if their feet hardly touched the ground, and at a great pace they bounded twenty feet in one step. It was a thrilling experience to witness this (few have seen the lung-gom-pa).

I was then given instruction and I felt as if my body was becoming light...

As my time was getting limited I moved on to Takohu Monastery, accompanied by Geshi Dar Tsang, and we received a cordial welcome from Geshi Tung La. His science was the art of reading the mind, otherwise known as telepathy.

Telepathy interested me very much, for here was something that I could use with effect in my own healing work, and I lost no time in getting down to real practice.

I developed an amazing power to read Geshi Tung La's mind, perhaps because we were very much in tune with each other, and I was interested in the work that I fell into it naturally.

While he spoke in Tibetan I spoke in Hindustani, to help to form our thoughts. I found it very simple---it came to me without effort.

Chapter VI

Geshi Tung La's explanation to me was like this: Thoughts make waves in the ether similar to radio waves. It is common knowledge that there is a multiple number of radio waves in the ether at the same time, and not one interferes with the other. These invisible waves become audible when you have an instrument to receive them. They are modified and transformed back into sound.

"Now," said Tung La, "man also has a broadcasting and a receiving set. The pituitary gland is the projecting organ, and the pineal gland is the receiving organ. Thought waves are sent out by one person to another person who, if he be in tune, will receive them. This must be done without effort. At the receiving end you must not try to interpret consciously; you must allow the feeling to come into the mind. This feeling is transformed into thought and you begin to know what is received.

"It is a sort of feeling, not really thinking, for thinking sets in motion the pituitary gland and this distorts the receiving mechanism of the pineal gland."

I found that this was true. When I tried to think what he was saying in Tibetan I could not get it completely, but, when I did not try, the whole formation of his thoughts was "received."

Tung La said: "You are a natural born receiver. Because you are a medium you speak from inspiration; you just speak without thinking!"

I replied: "That is perfectly true. If I thought what I was going to say, I would find myself floundering; but when I just speak as I feel, and feel as I speak, the flow is perfect."

"That is correct," he told me. "You do not need any instruction in telepathy, as you are a born medium for it. There are many like you---but few have found it out."

Chapter VI

I was pleased to hear his confirmation that I was a natural medium; I was reading the minds of others all the time, though I did no know it.

As I have already mentioned, I have healed people all over the world, many of whom could not speak a word of my language, nor I of theirs. When they spoke I took no heed of what they were saying but I got a clear picture of their complaint. Intuition, call it what you like, the fact that I knew what was in their minds, proved I could read their thought-feelings. In point of fact, their thoughts and feelings were transferred to me, and I could feel what they felt, according to their thought-feelings. I could tell if they were sincere or not, I would know if they liked me or not, I knew if they were doubtful or full of fear. All the shades of their thought-feelings were to be quite clear.

Anyway, I witnessed the pupils, over twenty in number, practising sending messages to one another. They were changed about, until he found the best pairs. The accuracy of their projecting and receiving was astounding.

Firstly, the projector would write a letter of the alphabet or a number on a board in front of him, and the other with his back to him would write it down.

Then a word would be written, then a sentence, then the projector would read silently out of a book while the receiver would repeat it, and a recorder standing by would write down as the receiver repeated the words. Very seldom did they make a mistake. I thought it was a wonderful demonstration. The distance between them was increased until a range of mountains separated them. It showed that there is no space, that we are not separated.

"Light and sound are carried by the ether waves," said Geshi Tung La, "so is thought and feeling."

I stayed here ten days and a grand friendship sprang up between us. He would speak in Tibetan, and I in Hindustani. We did this in general conversation also, to keep our practice up.

Several years later, in a seance in London, Geshi Tung La came through and spoke to me. He told me that he was still in his earthly body and was helping me in my work, as he had since learned astral travel from the hermit of Ling-Shi-La (of whom I will speak later).

"Yes," I thought, "there are greater things in Heaven and on earth than man has yet dreamed of."

The proof which I now had was conclusive, for nobody but myself knew that Tung La existed.

I often felt the telepathic influence of Geshi Tung La, just as I would feel the influence of other helpers whom I knew, including Geshi Rimpoche and my friend, but it never dawned upon me that Geshi Tung La could leave his body and work in the astral.

These thoughts came back to me from the words he spoke, before I left. He said "Love is the greatest magnetic force in the world; it is more powerful than the strongest magnet used to magnetise steel. When a piece of steel is magnetised, all the particles arrange themselves into north and south poles, harmonising the whole of the atoms in that piece of steel, and the steel then becomes a magnet itself. So does Love magnetise the etherons and atoms of the soul and body, turning them into a magnet to attract the Cosmic Rays in great abundance, thereby giving expression to the Love of God."

I said to him: "Yes, Jesus said, 'I have come that you may have Life and even more abundant Life."

For some time he sat in silence, and then he said: "You speak of the Master Jesus? We have records of him here; he is still with us."

Chapter VI

I sat up when he said this, for I knew that He was still the living Christ.

The deep impressions of Tung La's thoughts were made indelible to me; I can still feel the influence of the Love and affection he had for me.

And here let me tell you a truth. You can speak to each other without uttering a word when you are in tune. Try it sometime, and you will be amazed at the wonderful understanding you get. The result will be greater understanding of one another, a deeper feeling of love. It is said "Absence makes the heart grow fonder." It is because the thoughts which you send out to one another are being received.

May I continue to say here a few more words to you of that which I know to be true?

The harmonising of the atoms is based on the fundamental law upon which the function of Life is based---Love. This is the law of the electro-magnetic principle underlying all creation.

This principle is the basic power in creation throughout the Universe, not only on this planet but also in all the created Universe. Although it is not the Ultimate, this electro-magnetic principle is the motion in the Universe, and motion is the force that transforms the atoms of invisible matter into various visible forms, and Nature's subtle conductor is the ether.

In ether the blue-print of creation is formed, and motion causes the transformation of the etherons and atoms into form. This same ether remains the foundation of all forms throughout the whole of the electro-magnetic activity. This same rule applies throughout the whole Universe, because there is but one Creator and one creation: both are one and not separate. The Creator and His creation are one.

Ether is the conductor of Creative Thought, which is the most powerful activity, for by It the Universe is built.

I understood this when I was trained to be master of *prana yama*. To control the *prana* is to control phenomena and the dynamic forces in mind and body. Therefore, he who loves wins the love of God, but he who hates reaps what he sows.

Before I left Takohu Monastery my friend Tung La presented me with a small Tibetan prayer-wheel which I still have. It has been with me now for seventeen years, and it is fifteen years since I said that I would write this book.

I have been busy ever since, healing all over the world.

The last nine years were spent in South Africa and now, while I am on the ship en route to my old home in Scotland for a vacation, I am influenced to write this book, and another will follow soon.

Those who feel that they are guided by a greater force than their own desires know well that all things come at the right moment and not before or after.

This is not fatalism as some may think, but co-operation, a knowing that the Wisdom, the Intelligence that builds and controls the Universe, that same Power, must be in man, for man is the living expression of the Consciousness and Intelligence of God who guides and manifests all things according to His will, God being Infinite in Nature.

"Thy will be done, not mine, O Lord."

Now that I have said these few words to you, I will return to my story...

Chapter VI

As we were wending our way back, Dar Tsang left us when we came to Yangtang, and we kept on the same path, reaching the Chumbi Valley again, exactly three weeks and three days from the time we left.

I went straight to Geshi Rimpoche and told him all that had happened. He asked: "How did you like Tung La?" I replied: "He comes next to you and my friend in my heart."

Geshi Rimpoche then said: "I have word from him already; he tells me that you are an adept in telepathy and his regard for you is very strong."

I said: "So is mine for him."

"I am glad," he assured me.

Then I asked: "But how did you hear so soon?"

"Ah," he answered, "messages pass very quickly in Tibet; what you do now is known a hundred miles away in a very short time."

"I have already found that out," I said.

We talked long into the night about what I did and what I had learned, and, when he was satisfied that the journey was not in vain he said: "I am glad indeed at your successful sojourn, but you know it is not the Real. It is right that you should know the occult Sciences, but you realise that Truth is greater than all these things."

I said: "Yes, I do know that and it becomes clearer each day to me," and then I asked: "What about the hermits in the mountains, have they found the Truth?"

"No, my son," he replied, "you cannot find the Truth in the mountain or by the sea, nor by eating carrots, nor by concentrating on your umbilicus all day. Neither will you find it by running away from the world, because you are the world. There is no isolation, that is created only in man's mind, it is the great illusion. It is for this purpose that I have brought you here to make you see the false, then you will know what is the Real and the True. If you do not understand the false yourself, I cannot make you understand. You have been dabbling for years in the occult, that is why I want you to know the Real and the True thoroughly, so that you can be free."

"You will never understand, my son," he continued, "through a belief by mere meditation or suggestion; nor through the occult powers, nor in the future, nor in the past, can it be found, for the past is a memory and the future is hope mingled with fear. All these are of the mind, and Truth is beyond mind."

"Well," I said, "how do we arrive at the Truth?"

He answered: "I can only tell you the ways you cannot arrive at the Truth, and when you have found all the ways by which you cannot arrive at the Truth, you will find the Truth: then it will be yours, and not another's which is but an imitation."

He added: "You will not find it by mere analysis, for this is only digging up the past, and the Truth that sets you free is not of the past. When you see that the process of mere analysis is a false process you will discard it; it will drop from you like all the other false processes."

"What is in your mind," he continued, "is dead; it is not a living thing, but on the other hand Truth is that which is living from moment to moment. It must be discovered, not merely believed in, not to be quoted or formulated in the mind.

"To be alive, that is Truth; to know that you are Life and living every moment of It, that is Truth. To know this, your mind must be alert, aware, with your heart full of Love, free from all that is false; that is Truth."

"Most people," he went on, "do not want to be alive; they want to be put to sleep to escape the world, they do not want to face up to things; like children they want to hide behind their mother's apron strings, to shelter from the storm---and what is the storm? Is it not our relationship with one another? We must be conscious of that relationship every moment. But if I treat you like a piece of furniture there is no relationship between us. There is only true relationship when we understand ourselves; only then can there be freedom, and in freedom only is Truth revealed."

"If you love me and hate another can you" he asked, "claim to to know the Truth?" If you are kind to me and unkind to another, can you say that you are a kind person? Is it not the height of contradiction?"

I told him: "I have never seen it like this before."

"No, my son," he said, "that is because you did not understand yourself, your thoughts, your motives, your feelings, your cravings and from where and how they arose.

"When you get rid of all the things of the self, then only is the Truth known. It is only these false things that are preventing the Truth from flourishing in you. If your action is the contradiction of the Truth, how can you claim the Truth?"

"Then," he went on, "If you are influenced by your experience, by what is in your mind, you cannot give expression to that which is beyond your mind; you will be giving expression only to what is in your mind. What is in your mind is not the Truth. If your actions comes merely from your experience, then the Truth is not in you.

But if your actions arise from loving your neighbour as yourself, you will give expression to the Truth."

"Do you think that I am chastising you, my son?" he asked, gently... "Far from it, because my love for you is greater than for myself. You can now see that if the Truth you know is built upon what you have seen, heard, or read, then it will be superficial. In discovering the Truth you must search your mind to see what is false, and anything that you hold in your mind about the Truth is not the Truth. You become only a mere gramophone changing the records.

You must become the musician and the music at the same time, not merely listening to another.

Therefore, my son," he said, "you must understand the creations of the mind in reaction to others, to things external. You must see the falseness of these creations, for they are but ashes, not the Living Truth which cannot be destroyed, perverted, because It is not put together by the mind."

After he said this he remained silent---and I was silent too...Yes, my mind had undergone a change in that short space of time. What I had learned had passed into the background and Reality came to the fore. It was a queer feeling, similar to the one I had before, but it was stronger, a silence that was deeper; in a flash everything that I had read or heard of the Truth seemed to dissolve away. In that deep silence I knew, I did not know what it was, but I knew with a greater depth than ever before that I was the Truth, I was the living Truth *Now*, and nothing could destroy It, nor could anything destroy me, nothing could pervert the Truth. It was my own, not another's, Truth.

From here I could go on. I knew then that from that very moment I could go further, without effort or struggle. Previously the

Chapter VI

Truth was much to me a mental concept, and I could not face this fact because I did not want to let go of what I thought was true. But now I could face any fact, no matter what it was, good, bad or indifferent. I knew it could not alter the Truth---the Living Truth---that I knew myself to Be, and I knew that the Love that created me, created all. This was the Power given to man in heaven and on earth.

My thinking merged into the Silence from which arises Creative Thought, and as my confused thoughts dissolved away into nothingness I realised that which was not a mental concept. I had reached the Silence in which there was Perfect Love---beyond the human conception of Love.

This was not a dead silence as if I had been put to sleep, or a silence that I had created for myself; it was a silence when all confused thought, even thinking, ceased, and in that quiet, when the external no longer bound be, I found the creativeness, that is Eternal and Everpresent, and I knew I was one with It. It was mine *Now* and forever, and nobody could take It away from me. Love was the creative Power within all creation, because God is Love and all are One with Him, because there is none other than He.

It was Geshi Rimpoche who broke the silence. "Let us go out and see the sun set, my son," he said. I replied that I would like to do so; a sunset has never ceased to give me a thrill.

"It is a different sunset every night," I remarked.

"Yes," he answered, "I have looked at the sun setting and rising for many years now, and no two have ever been the same. It is the variety of the One Life, my son. You and I are of the same Life; the only difference is variety. When we understand variety we will know that 'One' alone is behind it all."

108

Chapter VI

Nothing uplifted me more than the words of Geshi Rimpoche; they had the effect of transforming my whole nature. It was not an intellectual knowing, but a deeper understanding and transformation that was taking place. I had found the source and I was content, content now to go on.

There was now no more searching or struggling; my searching and struggling to know what Truth was, had come to an end.

It was a moving onwards now that was necessary, and all that I would hear, see and feel, I knew would help me as it never did before; for while I thought before what was real, I now knew that it was not the Real---the "Uncreated" alone was Real and creative, not the created. This I knew, and what came after, although astounding, to say the very least, did not trouble me even if I did not know the "Why,'" for now I knew the cause behind all things, great and small, and I was one with it: it could not be otherwise, God being Infinite in Nature, and therefore there was no finite Being separate from the Infinite, for that would be impossible.

Afterwards, we had supper which had been specially prepared for my taste (chicken and roast potatoes) that previous similar meal that I have mentioned, had sunk into my subconscious because the relish in eating it when I was extremely hungry and having it in the open air, had given me physical satisfaction.

Then I said to Geshi Rimpoche: "I would like to hear first-hand from you about the people of Tibet, their habits and so forth--- anything that you kindly tell me will be of great personal interest, because my stay is necessarily short and my impressions of so vast a country must tend to be superficial."

"Yes, my son, you get my thoughts; I wanted to tell you something of the people and their habits, so that as you go along you will be better prepared to acquire the knowledge you would not otherwise get. But aren't you tired?" he asked.

"No," I replied, "an hour of this information from you would be very satisfying."

Then he said: "You have already found, I am sure, that the Tibetan people are a happy type."

"Yes," I agreed, "they are always laughing, especially the women I have met."

"Oh yes," he said, "they would be laughing, probably because they would like you for a husband, because of your being different from their own people."

I said: "I found that so. When we met about a dozen girls as we came into Yatung they started talking and laughing among themselves, and I asked my interpreter what they were saying. He told me that they were saying among themselves, 'nice husband.' One would say 'Mine,' and another would say 'Mine,' and they would all laugh heartily."

"Yes," he went on, "some of our people practise polyandry, but this is fast dying out.

Polyandry, as you know, means that the wife has more than one husband. If she marries the eldest son she accepts the younger sons in the family as well, and nobody knows who is the father of the children; the younger sons are called uncles. But if she marries the youngest son he becomes her only husband."

"But," I remarked, "there seem to be many more women than men."

"Yes," he agreed, "but that does not prevent them practising polyandry. Polygamy is practised too: some of the richer class have more than one wife, but this is also dying out."

"The infant mortality," he continued, "in Tibet is very high. Many of the mothers and babes die of the severe cold. In the outlying parts of Tibet when a lama doctor is not at hand the husband or neighbour becomes midwife. Sanitary arrangements are very crude, and a baby is lucky to get a bath---the baby is generally rubbed over with yak butter."

I remarked: "I suppose you have done a bit of mid-wifery in your time?"

"Oh yes, many times. In fact I got quite expert at it in my district," and he continued: "You can appreciate what hardships the mothers go through having children, for it is difficult enough to get fuel for cooking, let alone for heating water for a bath. Those who live near the woodline are more fortunate in being able to get wood, but they are more snowbound in the winter. So there is compensation both ways. Very seldom does a mother stay more than a day or so in bed."

I remarked: "I see a lot of girls hang about the monastery."

"Yes," answered Geshi Rimpoche, "although the lamas take a vow of celibacy some do not keep to the rule. In fact the abbots do not seem to care, and many of the children you see do not know who their father is. But Tibetans are passionately fond of children and, when a girl marries and has a child beforehand, the husband takes the child as his own; it bears his name and henceforth is known as his child."

I said: "That is very generous."

Chapter VI

"Well," he commented, "the people here do not look upon sex as you do in the West; they are happier as a result."

"Are there any divorces or anything like that?" I asked.

"Oh no," he said, "the lamas see to that," and he added:

"It is very desirable that a male child is born into the family, expecially when an estate is concerned. There is one man I know who married three sisters in the one family before he got a male child."

"Does he still keep the three wives?"

"Oh yes," he replied, "that is the rule."

"And they do not fight?"

"No, when people are brought up in this way they take it as a matter of course."

"It would not do for women in the West," I remarked.

"No," he said "but one does not know what the other is doing in the West, while they do know here, and it is that which makes all the difference."

"Quite a thought!" I said.

"There are cases where the father and the son have married the same woman, when the woman was not the son's mother."

"Oh," I exclaimed, "that is strange."

"Yes," he said, "but it does not often happen."

Chapter VI

"In polyandrous marriages," he continued, "the wife exercises great control over her household, for women have much influence in Tibet, both in the home and in business. They are exceedingly charming to meet, and very pleasing in their manner. They have an easy freedom that is not found in other parts of the world. Unlike the wives and daughters of other Asiatics, they always join visitors at tea and in fact are capable in looking after the husband's affairs.

There are great number of women traders in the towns and villages, and they are every bit as good as the men and many much better."

"In the West," I said, "they are getting that way too."

"The peasant women," he went on, "labour in the fields, attending to the ploughing and to the work on the land just as efficiently as the men. In fact the women are equal in every respect to their male folk."

"Men and women," he continued, "very seldom display jealousy when husbands and wives display interest in another, and it is considered no disgrace for a girl to have a child before marriage."

I said, "How do they manage to arrange these polyandrous marriages?"

"Well," he replied, "the husband that is in the room with the wife leaves his boots outside the door." We both laughed at this.

I said: "That is a good arrangement anyhow, but I do not think it would do in the West.

Neither polygamy nor polyandry would be tolerated. In fact, it is against the law to have two wives or two husbands."

"Yes," he replied, "I know that, for I have travelled in many countries in my younger days. You see my father was a Maharajah and I was sent to an English school in India. It was then that I met the Yogi who gave me an insight into the mysteries of Life. He advised me to see the world and understand it. I was a capable student and became an abbot, that is, a teacher in a Tibetan monastery. I have learned most of the occult Sciences including Tumo."

"Yes, I heard that you were a Master of Tumo as well."

"Yes," he said, "The powers of man are hidden from the unenlightened, and it is by the wisdom of the Creator that only those who have the understanding can use them."

"Yes," I told him, "I am grateful for the opportunity of being taught by the masters of the various occult Sciences, and all this is due to your great interest in me."

When I said this he looked upon me as a father would look upon a son he loved.

Time passed quickly and it was almost midnight.

"Now," he said "you must retire, I will tell you more about Tibetan people to-morrow, but you will see much for yoursef on your way to Ok Valley. You know your friend is waiting for you there, and you must leave Lingmatang soon."

"I have grown to like Lingmatang; I feel it is my home," I said.

"It is," he said, "it is your home any time you want to come; the door will always be open to you."

This was grand to hear from such a great sage as Geshi Rimpoche, for it was sincere. I felt happy and turned in for the

114

remainder of the hours left for rest, looking forward to what the dawn would bring.

CHAPTER VII

When I got up next morning I was still intrigued with what Geshi Rimpoche had told me and was eager to hear more. I went to the window and could see Rimpoche standing on the balcony. He was looking towards the east where the sun would soon rise.

It was dark, and a dark cloud like a dark blanket covered the valley, looking sinister. I had not seen Tibet like this before and I was wondering what was going to happen, when I heard a clap of thunder, which echoed backwards and forwards, up and down the valley.

Closed in as it was by the mountains, it sounded like a volley of big guns in quick succession.

As yet it had not started to rain, so I went out on the balcony where Geshi Rimpoche was. He was deep in contemplation.

He said: "I was just thinking of the many moods of Nature takes on. Last night the stars were shining brightly, without a cloud in the blue sky, and now the whole valley and hills are filled with dark menacing clouds, ready to burst at any minute, swelling the rivers into roaring torrents."

"Yes," I replied, "It is truly wild this morning," and then another louder clap of thunder burst around us. The lighting struck the face of the great rock about one hundred yards away, we heard the report as if a thousand million volts had struck it, and the flash burst around us. I said, "It is a good thing that it did not strike the monastery."

"Yes," he concurred, "but in no time in memorable history has a monastery been hit by lighting."

Just then the clouds burst. I never saw anything like it.

Chapter VII

It was not rain, it was as if sheets of water were poured down from giant vessels. The river below began to roar with the torrents, nearly as loud as the thunder.

"I hope this does not last long," I said.

He agreed, and added: "Nature is in a nasty mood but she will change soon."

No sooner had he said this than I could see a break in the clouds where the sun was just peeping from behind the great Himalayas that surrounded us, and it was not long before the storm ceased, and immediately there was a calm.

"You see," he said, "that is the nature of this land of mountains and rivers."

The sun was coming up with an array of colours, entirely different from the usual sight, and the sky held a wild dark sinister beauty. It seemed as if I was transported from one world to another in a few minutes for, as the sun rose, the dark menacing clouds melted away and a beautiful blue sky appeared.

"Well," I remarked, "I have never seen such a quick change before," and he observed: "This is a country of contrasts."

Afterwards we had breakfast. I had two boiled eggs and toast and tea, and Rimpoche just had some tsampa, a sort of baked bread, and tea, and then we went out again upon the balcony and sat down.

"I would like to hear more about the people and their ways," I told him.

He recalled that he had been telling me about the marriage customs and social features of the people there.

Chapter VII

"What about the fashions?" Do these change at all?" I inquired.

"Oh no," he replied, "there is no change of fashion here. Men and women wear the same type of clothes now as of hundreds of years ago; there is no change.

Very dull, I thought. "It would not do for the changeable moods of the West," I remarked.

"No," he said, just as if in answer to my thought, "but the fact is that the style of the Tibetan dress has not changed for centuries," and he continued: "A great contrast exists between the dress of the lower classes and that of the upper classes in appearance, style and quality. This is according to the laws of the country, and these laws regulate the quality and colour of the garments of each class."

I could not help asking: "Do the people no object to be told what to wear?"

"Oh no," he answered, "all this has been the custom for centuries. The costume for women of rank is most attractive; even when they are engaged in domestic things the ladies never neglect their personal appearance. Every woman delights in loading herself with jewellery and ornaments. Around their necks you have no doubt seen charm boxes hanging?"

"Yes," I said, "nearly everyone has them, young or old, rich or poor."

"And," he continued, "in their charm boxes there is a prayer--- they believe that this protects them from evil. For the upper classes these charm boxes are made of gold and studded with precious jewels; and if the agate beads on which the boxes hang around the neck have certain markings these are considered lucky; they are of great value. And on their clothes they hang pieces of their best jade.

119

Some wear, down their back, a special piece of brocade into which are set precious stones, some of them worth thousands of pounds."

"On their fingers," he went on, "they wear gold rings set with jewels or with their favourite lucky stone. Earrings of jade are always worn. Yet nowhere in the world will you see such indifference to, such disregard for, filth.

I have seen ladies dressed in the most gorgeous costumes walking along the road with their garments trailing in dirt which I would hesitate to put my horse through. You will see for yourself this morning how some of these ladies are dressed."

He then told me that he was to officiate at an important wedding of leading lights of the district that day, "and I want you to come with me. I have arranged with the bridegroom's parents that you will be given the seat of honour, from which you will see everything."

So we journeyed down to the village, and from where I stood I could see the bride astride a gaily decorated pony coming towards the bridegroom's house.

Around her head was a gaily-coloured scarf and I asked: "What is the scarf for?"

"Oh," replied Geshi Rimpoche, "that is to hide her blushes."

Refreshments were set at three selected places, quite near each other and close to the house; cakes were made at each of the three places and the bride and her party sampled them.

When she reached the gate of the bride-groom's house, someone threw into her face a "torma,' which is a dagger made by the lamas from barley dough and butter cooked hard and painted red.

I said: "That does not seem a very nice thing to do," and Geshi Rimpoche explained: "It is supposed to drive away any evil spirit that has come with her."

"It's a nice way to meet a bride!" I laughed.

The bride was met at the gate by the bridegroom and his mother. The mother put upon the bride's head an arrow with the streamers of the five sacred colours. I asked why, and he replied: "It means acceptance by the mother and it is much thought of as her marriage licence. In fact it is the only marriage licence that some ever get."

They all now entered the house, and the bride sat at the right hand of the bridegroom.

Friends and relatives laid their gifts at their feet.

Then Geshi Rimpoche put round both their necks a scarf of silk and pronounced them man and wife, and then the mother came and placed another scarf round the bride's and bridegroom's neck. This ended the marriage ceremony, and all adjourned to the marriage feast which would go on till late in the evening.

I partook of some of the food, and there were about sixteen courses consisting of all kinds of sweetmeats and plenty of barley beer, which is turned on *ad lib.* Before long I could see that many could hardly sit on their chairs, let alone stand.

We then left, because Geshi Rimpoche had another mission. This was to a girl who married the elder brother thinking that by so doing she would get the younger one with whom she was in love. But to her great sorrow the younger brother refused to have anything to do with the marriage.

"I heartily agree with him," I said, "and what are you going to do about it?"

Chapter VII

"You will see," he told me.

We reached the house, and there, sitting on the porch, was a girl looking into space as if she were in a dream. She started when she saw us, and came down and kissed the hem of Geshi Rimpoche's garment. He placed his hand upon her head, blessing her, and he said, in Tibetan, "Arise, my daughter, and be at peace."

I was struck by her beauty; she was truly a comely Tibetan girl. Her eyes were well set apart, her nose was straight and her mouth firm, her lips were beautifully formed. When she laughed she showed a beautiful set of faultless teeth. Her name was Norbu, which means beautiful jewel. The name suited her.

The name of Tibetans, Rimpoche told me, were those of places or things, such as beautiful mountain, beautiful valley, flowers, jewels, and the like. All these names were chosen for their meaning.

There had been no children by the marriage, and this was a severe blow to Norbu. If there is anything in the world Tibetan women want it is children; to them a childless marriage is no marriage at all and it can be annulled by themselves.

This particular girl became agitated when she asked Rimpoche about Tang La (which means a level pass). Tang La was the younger brother. There was a tremor in her voice as she spoke of him. She said: "I do not understand why he will not come home," and tears welled up in her big blue eyes.

Geshi Rimpoche replied: "He is in love with you, Norbu, but he is unwilling to share you with his brother."

"I will go to him," she said.

Chapter VII

"All right, my daughter, go to him. He is over in Darjeeling. The Himalayas separate you; do you think you can make such a journey, my daughter?"

"Oh yes," and she went inside. Later I heard that she had crossed the Himalayas and got to Darjeeling, where they were married again by the local Buddhist priest. A few months later I asked Geshi Rimpoche about her. She had made an impression on me, for it was rare Tibetan love story. Geshi told me that they were happy and Norbu was going to have a child and she was extremely beautiful and radiant.

He added: "I knew that the bond of love between them would work out satisfactorily; a true bond always does."

"What about the elder brother?" I inquired.

"Oh," he replied, "that has been settled quite satisfactorily, and he is married again."

I thought to myself: "Well, this is a peculiar country indeed."

We visited another home, where a man was dying, and Geshi Rimpoche had been sent for by the relatives. The man died not long after we arrived. The presence of Geshi Rimpoche had a soothing effect upon the whole scene. I never saw anything like it. It was as if a new life had come into being, and everyone went about his or her work knowing all was well.

I asked: "And what happens now?"

"Oh," he replied, "to-morrow or the next day he will be taken to the burial ground."

"So," I inquired, "they bury them here too?"

Chapter VII

"Oh no, not the way you bury people in the West. Do you see the vultures up there on the hillside?"

"Yes."

"Well, those vultures are waiting to eat the flesh off the man's body. The people you see up on the hill are called the Ragypa. They are outcasts, and they cut up the flesh of the dead and throw it to the vultures. The bones are thrown to the dogs, until all is devoured. There is nothing left. That is what happens to ordinary people."

I said that I would like to see it.

"Do you think you would? It is a gruesome sight."

"Well," I said, "I can only imagine what it is like if I don't see it."

"All right then, let us go---there is always someone's body being devoured."

So we went up the side of the hill to the place which they called "Skulls," and I watched the awesome procedure. First they stretched a body out on a platform and in no time with their sharp knives they had cut off all the flesh clean to the bone, and as they cut they threw the pieces to the vultures.

The pieces were quickly devoured by the shrieking flesh-eaters who flew down almost pecking the pieces out of the Ragypas' hands.

It was a sickening sight. (The peculiar thing about these gruesome scenes is that the vultures will not eat till the king vulture takes the first piece.)

Chapter VII

Then the bones were broken up and given to the dogs. Several heads that had been separated from the bodies were strewn around. The Ragypas break up the skulls, and pick out the eyes and the brain and throw these to the vultures; the skull they reduce to powder and the relatives can have it if they wish---if not, the dogs eat it.

"It was a sickening sight," I said to Geshi Rimpoche, "but I was glad I saw it."

"You must see things as they are, my son, without repulsion, otherwise you are not free."

I said: "That is true; I have still a lot to free myself from yet."

"Now," he informed me, "the general rule is for a lama to go to the house of the dead man and perform what is known as the cleansing ceremony."

"Oh," I said, "that is interesting."

"Would you like to see that too?"

"Yes," I replied, "I may as well see the whole thing. I have seen the marriage, the death and the burial and now the cleansing ceremony---the only thing that will complete the human cycle is to see a birth, and then I will have the whole picture of the ways of the Tibetans---birth, life, death."

He said: "I expect there will be a lama there now." So we went back to the house and surely enough the lama was there. He had not yet begun the cleansing ceremony and he at once made way for Geshi Rimpoche to do it, but Geshi Rimpoche waved to him to continue.

There was quite a lot to it. The lama drew on a piece of paper an effigy of the deceased and burnt it, all the time watching it intently.

125

If it burnt bright the soul would have reached the highest Heaven; if red and spread out, the soul had departed from the house. If it burnt smoky the soul was still around the house. Then the lama besought the soul to depart from the house and not trouble the household any more, telling him that he would find his resting place where he would await the time when he could reincarnate.

I said to Geshi Rimpoche: "One thing I like about it is that the people understand there is no death, but this paper-burning business is, according to the paper used, just superstition."

"You are right, my son, but it gives comfort to those who are left; they believe it; they are not yet sufficiently advanced to understand the Truth as we understand it."

I said: "I can see quite clearly that there are people who need a religion until they have progressed enough to understand what is false; then they will realise what is true."

"Now, my son, you have seen the death, the burial and the cleansing of the house of the ordinary man. But with the high lamas the procedure is quite different. Their bodies are preserved in vaults over which is built a tomb plated in solid gold and studded with precious gems, and in the inner sanctum there are golden images and rich brocades beyond price. The contrast is so great that one can hardly imagine it possible. You have seen some of these tombs in the monasteries, but really to see something you must visit the Dalai Lama's tomb."

"Yes," I answered, "before I leave I must see the Dalai Lama's tomb, and then I asked him: "Why is it that the few high officials who are allowed to enter Tibet do not inquire into the real things of Life instead of scraping on the surface about the things that do not matter?"

"My son," he replied, "you know the answer yourself; you do not need me to tell you that."

I did not say anything, but I thought to myself that his reply was very true; it was stupid to ask the question. I know well enough why---it is because they do not know anything about the Real, being steeped in the false. People who live on the surface can see only what is on the surface. How they could have missed the Real in Life is a human tragedy.

We were silent for a time---I had my thoughts and he had his. I think these were much on the same plane, for Geshi Rimpoche said: "My son, you must be on your way the day after to-morrow. To-morrow you can prepare and rest for the strenuous journey. I feel that your friend is calling you."

I replied: "I know that, but how can I pull myself away from here?"

"These are things we must learn to do, my son. There are times when you would like to remain where you are happy, but, remember, you are needed elsewhere. When you took on this work you were content to go where you were needed."

"Yes, I know that," I said. "I have found that in many places I would have liked to stay but the power of the Spirit is stronger than the flesh, so I moved on."

* * * * * * *

I often wonder why I did not write this book before I wrote *The Higher Power You Can Use* first, then *I am the Life,* then *Heal Yourself,* then *Spiritual and Mental Healing,* then *What is Mine is Thine* (two parts), then *How to Relax and Revitalize Yourself,* then *Divine Healing of Mind and Body* (the Master speaks again), then

Chapter VII

Your Life renewed every Day --- and now this book *Beyond the Himalayas.*

When I look back I can see a sequence running through all these books. They seemed to come without any planning on my part, and yet they dovetailed into each other.

As I have said, I will, D.V., write another book similar to this as the space left here would not be sufficient for what I have yet to tell. I could imagine Geshi Rimpoche saying: "Yes, my son, you will go on writing as long as you live on the physical plane."

The morning came for my departure. I said a temporary goodbye to Geshi Rimpoche, and I could see by his face the affection he had for me, and I am sure he felt mine also.

I turned from him and walked away down the steps of the monastery into the valley below. I looked back several times and there he was, standing on the spot where I left him.

Audibly to myself I said: "No wonder everyone loves you, Geshi Rimpoche; you have everything that a friend needs in a friend--- Love, compassion, wisdom, understanding, kindness and forgiveness."

Once when I said to him that I was sure I had often been a worry to him, he replied: "Oh no, my son, I know that the flesh is weak but the Spirit is strong and must in the end succeed and find its freedom. It is because you know these weaknesses yourself that you are tolerant to others---you could not be a healer otherwise. You must neither condemn nor judge, for who are we that we may condemn or judge? What we see in others is deeply rooted in ourselves."

I have never forgotten his words. By them I knew the greatness of the man.

Chapter VII

When we reached the valley, the monastery was nearly out of sight. A feeling of loneliness took hold of me in the Ok Valley. He would have much of interest to say to me, I was sure.

We left Lingmatang behind and followed the track on to a place called Gautsa, where there was a hut, about twelve miles from Lingmatang, and here we stayed the night. The going was very rough, the river was in a spate because of the melting snows in the mountains and it was rushing like mad through the gorges. We had to make our own way down the mountain track to the river-side. It was hard going because of the steep side of the mountains; some of which were sheer precipices all the way down. Eventually we reached the stony track along the side of the swollen river which in places was dangerously near the track. Overhanging the river in parts were thick bushes of wild roses and other flowers that made a grand picture.

I had taken a good number of snaps by this time and was almost tired of taking them, because it was so difficult to choose from among the many wonderful sights. When I saw a beautiful scene I would say to myself that perhaps there would be an even better one farther on.

This is what happens when there is so very much to take in.

On the side of the mountain I could see several lama hermitages and I remembered what Geshi Rimpoche had told me: "You cannot find the Truth by isolation and such like." So I went on my way; sometimes I was tempted to stop and have a look, but I kept going, as time was limited.

We left the river-bed again and climbed the mountain track once more, but the going up and down made it tiresome travelling. Then we came on a clearing from which we could see the plain through the trees. The plain was green with thick grass and yaks were there in their hundreds grazing. Wild flowers were prolific, contributing to another scene of beauty, and I wondered whether I could get such beauty on a film. I thought, no! Yet I took the picture later and can see it in my mind now as fresh as the day I took it.

Then we entered the wildest scenery: the contrast was almost too much to realise. The track now was not more than two to three feet wide going round the mountainside and skirting the gorges through which the river roared. At times we came upon an opening where we could see again this beautiful valley in the distance coloured with wild flowers, with a large number of yaks grazing. I could see the hut in which we were to put up for the night on the other side of the river, and I realise that from it I should be able to see more of this lovely carpeted as it was with such colourful wild flowers. We came to a bridge suspended over the river, and we crossed very gingerly. I was tired by the end of the day, though it was not a long journey (I had done nearly twice as far before), but in this particular stretch there was so much climbing to do--we would climb down to the river side, then up again, and so on.

After supper, which was an enjoyable one (I always enjoyed my food after the day's journey), my bearer played some tunes on his accordion. When I went to bed I could not help thinking of what had happened to me in the short time I had been there, and I had almost to pinch myself to see if it was not a dream. Had all this really happened?

What I had seen and heard during the last few weeks would fill a book by itself, but that would be of little use to you who want to study my books; if you want more than a mere description of what I saw, you want to know more about Life and what it means.

All through my travels in Tibet I came across many prayer-flags. At every dangerous place there would be a prayer-flag---a prayer for the traveller that his feet would be kept safe on the dangerous paths or that the mountain would not roll down upon him. Yes, I thought, these people were thoughtful. Many would laugh at these prayer-flags, but I did not, for I knew that with every flag there was a thought for the safety of the one who passed that way.

Next day we travelled as far as Phari Dzong. As we left the gorges we entered into the great expanse of pastures of which we had caught glimpses the day before. It was a beautiful fertile valley, and hundreds of yaks were grazing among the wild flowers. Here was another yak train carrying more wool over the mountains to India.

When I thought of India it seemed to be a thousand miles away, another world, an outside world. In the distance we could now see Phari, reputed to be the highest town in the world (and the filthiest). Phari is 15,000 feet above sea level.

Eventually we came to the hut just outside Phari on the edge of the valley, and here we put up for the night.

We had the usual evening meal and my bearer played his accordion. Next morning we had the usual breakfast and were soon off again.

We now enter Phari. How could I explain it to you? Around it is the most beautiful green pasture, coloured with wild flowers, even more beautiful in some respects than the Chumbi Valley. All kinds of animals were grazing there, yak, Tibetan sheep and goats; birds of all kinds flew around, whistling as if to welcome us; and there were little animals which I had never seen before, I learned that these were mostly mouse hares and that they live under the ground in burrows.

In all this grandeur Phari itself was a blot of filth. No rubbish could have been removed for centuries; the people just threw their offal and rubbish outside the door, and with the frost and the snow accumulations had mounted up so high that you could barely see the tops of the houses. Of sanitary arrangements there was none, so everyone squatted in the street; men, women and children left behind their droppings. I could barely believe it possible.

They never wash themselves; the only wash they ever got was with rancid yak butter, and you could see it deeply caked on their clothes.

As you can understand, I was glad to move out of Phari. I was now on my way to Ok Valley. My spirits soared again, for I would see my friend once more, my friend who had met me first in Kalimpong and who knew more about me than I knew myself.

I realised that I had some wonderful friends, natural friends not supernatural, for there is no such thing as a supernatural person, as Geshi Rimpoche told me. The idea of a supernatural person has come from the belief that there are two kinds of people, natural and supernatural, but it is not so; what seems to be supernatural is perfectly natural when understood. This I had already learned. No wonder that I did not want to leave, but it was not to be. I must go back into the world where I would be more useful, I was told, for I could do what they could not do in the circumstances, they said.

Their deep knowing was almost beyond human understanding. The words of Jesus came into my mind, "Believe in me and in *Him* who sent me."

We proceeded now at a faster pace down to Ok Valley, across one of the stormiest passes in Tibet where the wind blew the stones up into your face.

Chapter VII

The wind was blowing fiercely; it seemed to rise out of the calm to become a hurricane, and out of the storm comes the calm again. What a contrast, I thought.

The icy blasts were now coming from the frozen atmosphere of Chomolhari, and I felt my face freezing, and my fingers were becoming numb.

"And this is the middle of summer!" I asked by bearer.

"He answered: "It gets warmer as the sun rises, Sahib.""

"It would need to," I remarked "otherwise I would have to practise Tumo."

This day the beautiful Chomolhari was seen at its best.

Nearly ten miles away, as the crow flies, it looked as if it was falling on top of us.

We took the track to the right, just a few miles over the top of the pass which led to Ok Valley. The track passed a small lake that reflected the snow-capped Chomolhari and beyond was a river which we would have to cross; beyond that there was a small range of mountains that hid the lower part of Chomolhari. Its magnificent peak was covered with the eternal snows.

Chomolhari was showing itself in all its glory that day.

The sun was up but had not lost some of its orange colour which reflected from the snow. This created an illusion that Chomolhari might fall on us any minute. I stood, I don't know how long, drinking in this rare and beautiful sight hidden away from the outside world.

Chapter VII

The path was easy going, though over 15,000 feet above sea level. We had not gone more than a few miles when we saw in the distance another familiar but lovely scene. There, tucked away on the steep side of the mountain, was perched the great monastery of Ok Valley.

"How in all the earth are we to reach that place?" I asked, "and what a view of Chomolhari they must have, morning, noon and night. All the moods of Nature can be seen from here."

No sooner had I said this to my bearer than I saw my friend only a hundred yards away. The greeting I received from him was one of tender feeling, the love of a friend that is more than a friend.

He said: "I have followed you all the way to Yangtang, to Gonsaka and Takohu. You have made a deep impression on Dar Tsang, Malapa and especially Tang La."

"How do you know all this?" I asked.

"I was there, my son."

I had forgotten for the moment that moving about in the Astral was as easy to him as breathing was to me.

He said: "This is a beautiful spot, and we can do much here. The view you will have of the mountain at sunset and sunrise will compensate for the cold. But I forgot, you have learned something of Tumo now, so it will not be so bad for you," he said with a smile.

I laughed and said: "I hope that is true, and this will be a good test."

"What I want to do here," he went on, "is to make you more proficient in your inspiration, especially from the highest Spiritual

Forces, and here is the most suitable place as it is so high and secluded."

I replied: "I know I am better at thought transference now."

"Yes," he said, "but this is much more difficult. It is over-shadowing. It is much more perfect and reliable way of getting a message over, because there is more direct contact. Also your mind must be empty and free from fixed ideas, otherwise you will be colouring what is said with what is in your own mind."

"You see," he continued, "it is impossible to take complete control of you brain; we would have to take you out of your body to use your brain, and this is not suitable because of the tremendous Spiritual power that would be used. It would not be right for us to do that to you; your mechanism is too valuable to us to harm it."

I smiled and said: "I am flattered when you say that."

"Not so," he told me, "you are a medium of a certain kind that is rare; you were born that way, for this work you were born."

"I have heard that before," I commented.

"Yes, and you will hear it again." He was serious and added: "We want to see how much spiritual power you can stand and if we are successful you will be used by the Master himself."

"Good God," I exclaimed, "I am not worthy."

"Perhaps not," he replied, "but you have been chosen."

"If that is so, then I shall submit to any test you may put upon me."

By this time we had reached the monastery.

Chapter VII

"What if all this was written? It would make queer reading. No one would believe it," I said.

He answered: "The ignorant would not believe it, the bigoted would not believe it, but it is not for them; it is for those who are just beyond the physical, and for those who on earth are chosen to hear it and to see it. What is said will be taken down and not a word will be lost."

It is now, I realise the importance of his words, for otherwise the book *Divine Healing of Mind and Body* (The Master speaks again) would never have been written.

I had noticed, that we had climbed the steep grade to the monastery itself, and when I looked back and saw how far we had come I said, with a surprised look: "Good gracious, I had no idea that we had reached this height!"

With that he smiled, knowing more than I did.

CHAPTER VIII

The monastery of Ok was similar in every respect to Yangtang. I was given quarters next to my friend. It was an abbot's spare apartment, consisting of a sleeping room, another room with cushions, and the floor was covered with Tibetan rugs which made it look cosy and comfortable.

Plenty of water was obtained from a stream which came from the snows higher up and passed the side of the monastery.

After a wash and clean up I was introduced to a young Tibetan, not more than twentyfive years of age, called Tsang Tapa. He had a very intelligent face, and he was the oracle of the monastery. He was found by Geshi Rimpoche in a way that sounds like a fairy tale, as it was told to me by Geshi Rimpoche himself, and this is it.

When Geshi Rimpoche was on one of his journeys he came upon Tsang Tapa, who was then only fifteen years old, and it was away in a valley behind Mount Everest. Geshi Rimpoche had not eaten any food for days and was not likely to get any, when this young boy, Tsang Tapa, appeared from nowhere and offered him food and drink. Tsang Tapa then went straight into a trance and the great saint Malarepa spoke through him, demonstrating before Geshi Rimpoche the miraculous powers Tsang Tapa possessed.

To Geshi Rimpoche there was no doubt that the one who spoke through this lad was the real Malarepa himself---the great miracle worker. After the trance state was over, the boy said that he had been told that Rimpoche was coming this way and would be without food, so he, Tsang Tapa, brought food. The young boy then took Geshi Rimpoche down a secret path and here before them was a magnificent valley in which were grazing a large number of yak. Geshi asked the boy whose yaks they were and he said: "Mine, master."

This was strange, and Geshi asked: "Where are your parents?"

"They are far away, master."

Geshi was so interested now that he asked Tsang Tapa how he got here.

"O," replied the boy, "I move this way, master," and he started to do the lung-gom-pa.

This was most extraordinary. How could a young boy do the lung-gom-pa? So Geshi Rimpoche asked him: "Who taught you?"

"Him, master."

"Who is 'him'?"

The boy again said "Him," as if there were someone with him. Geshi knew at once that here was the most wonderful natural medium he had ever come across. So he took him to a great Yogi in Kalimpong district whom he knew.

For seven years the boy had been with this Yogi and during the last three years he had been the oracle at Ok. His rank was now greater than that of the Abbot.

I was so taken up with this story that I spoke to Tsang Tapa in Hindustani and he replied to me in English. I was more than surprised.

Apparently, while he was with the Indian Yogi, this Yogi sent him to an English school in Kalimpong, where he learned so quickly that the others could not keep up with him. I confirmed it afterwards that Tsang Tapa was indeed a most remarkable young man. His mediumship was extraordinarily clear and accurate. We also became good friends. His mediumship brought near to me many who had passed from the physical, so accurately that there was no doubt whatever about the identity of those who spoke.

I was introduced to the Abbot who was in charge of the monastery. He, too spoke English, so conversation was easy now and I did not need any interpreters. The Abbot was a jolly fellow and kept us laughing. Indeed I could not help laughing because his laughter was so infectious.

I had brought with me some one-pound tin boxes of Huntley & Palmers' biscuits which were relished by all four of us. I could not have brought anything better. We had tea, and ate sparingly of the biscuits because we wanted them to last.

The food in the monastery was very good, consisting of yak meat, barley, potatoes and tsampa, plenty of yak butter, milk, cream and cheese. Roast chicken and roast potatoes were available at least once, sometimes twice, a week.

When evening was drawing near I said I wanted to see the sun setting on Chomolhari, so we went out on the top of the main hall. The roof was flat and from it we could see the valley below, and beyond was Chomolhari.

I can only try to explain what I saw in words which cannot adequately paint a picture of such beauty.

The sun was setting behind us and on the side of Chomolhari. The colouring of pink I could not completely describe, for I had never seen anything like it anywhere else in the world.

As the pink gave way to the darker reds, a purple haze rose up from the valley. Gradually the purple haze became darker in colour and eventually turned into a cloud, creeping up and covering the mountain bit by bit until just the peak was reflecting the glowing red of the sun.

Chapter VIII

Then the peak disappeared and before us, covering the whole valley and the mountain, was a glorious blanket colour from purple to red, and in-between were all the other shades of the spectrum. (This is a poor description because words fail.)

The sunrise was equally beautiful but the colouring was in the opposite direction; the blanket began to dissolve as the sun rose, revealing the same colour formation in reverse.

It was a thrilling, an unforgettable experience.

We were up before the sun rose each day, for there was much to do. At first I did not know the procedure, but I felt quite content that all would be well and successful.

My friend took on the robe of the teacher. His wisdom and knowledge were profound.

He and Geshi Rimpoche were on the same plane.

My friend began to speak in his clear tones and I knew that he had something very important to say. We all listened intently.

He said: "Truth is not created in the mind. What people do is to create a religion that dominates them, a civilisation that exploits them, and because they do no understand they want something to guide them. Then they become slaves."

I looked at Tsang Tapa to see how he was taking it especially about his religion. My friend must have read my thoughts, for he said: "Never mind Tsang (as he called him); he shed the shackles of slavery long ago."

I was on the point of asking Tsang something when my friend continued: "Most people hold an ideal of unity while they hold fast to their divisions and separations. They refuse to give up their creeds, their nationalities, their religious beliefs, their political differences, because they are bound up with them, thereby failing to see that they are false. Anything that separates man from man, whether it be a religion, a nationality, an ideal, a belief, must be false because there is no division in Reality."

"Now," he continued, "they say you must pray---meditate---to find peace, to find freedom. So they meditate upon an idea of peace, of freedom, which binds them still further.

Without knowing how they are bound by what is in their minds, and how it has been formulated, their meditation, their prayers, are useless. When they do not know what causes separation, then unity, peace, freedom or whatever name they give it, will be merely an idea."

I said: "You speak almost like Geshi Rimpoche."

"My son," he replied, "there is only one way to freedom and that is to show how one is bound. I cannot free you; you must do that yourself. Only then will you find the mighty creative power that is behind all creation, the Love and the Wisdom that is beyond your mind.

Yet your mind is the vehicle through which it will manifest. How can it manifest through a mind that is filled with all that which is false? You would be expressing your own conditioning, not the Love, the Wisdom and the Power of the Christ Spirit."

He continued: "It is for this that I have brought you here. Your mind must be made clear enough for the over-shadowing of the Master, otherwise you would be giving expression to your own conditioning. Even after you leave here, your mind will not be completely ready for what we want to do. It will mean years of probationary work for you among the people of the world. What we are doing is preparing you, by showing you that what is made up in the mind is not Truth. The experience of seeing this in your everyday work will do more to cleanse your mind than if you stayed here twice as long. When you are working in the world we shall be helping you, and not only you but also the people whom you are helping."

Again, I said: "There are greater men than I in the world whom the people would heed more than they would heed me."

He said: "My son, for this you were born."

I asked: "But surely we were not destined so accurately as this?"

He answered: "Did not the Master say that not a sparrow falls to the ground but the

Father knoweth?"

I was stumped every time, but I thought I would fire a last shot.

"Well," I said, "I am not free to do as I please."

"Oh yes," he answered, "you are not compelled, you are only impelled. But that impelling becomes your innermost desire."

"In that event," I said, "I would like nothing better than to do this work, no matter where it takes me."

"Then let us proceed, and when your mind is somewhat clearer we will be able to get down to some practical work, which I want to commence as soon as possible."

He continued: "As long as you retain your conception of even individuality there can be no release from the conflict of relationship. So true meditation, true prayer, is to find out what is false, not merely concentraTing on an idea while ignorant of the cause of conflict which continues to reign in and about you.

"People repeat certain phrases which you call mantrims, by doing this they think they are meditating or praying, but this is merely self-hypnosis. Meditation is not devoted to an idea, and the worshipping of another is idolatrous and silly superstition. To be devoted to an idea, to a picture, is not meditation, it is merely an escape from oneself. It is perhaps a comforting escape, but still it is an escape without understanding. The world is the people and the people are the world; then you are the world, I am the world, is that not so?"

I replied: "Yes, that is true, the world is just as we make it. We made this civilisation by which we are dominated."

"Right," he said, "the people are slaves because they have made themselves slaves.

They follow, they imitate, they set up authorities, while tradition, belief, division in society, nationalities, have bound the mind in thought and emotion. The individual has merely conformed while in his world of action he has built for himself a false security."

"I can see that clearly," I said, "for there is no security in the relative world, it is an illusion."

"Yes," he said, "people are constantly striving to become virtuous, and they are caught up in the process which denies understanding. Controlling your mind is an unnecessary effort, which brings fear and limitation, because your mind is dominated by the idea of an escape from your conditioning which you fear."

"What happens when an idea comes into your mind," he reasoned, "do you not try to brush it aside so as to escape from its influence? But its influence still remains because it is not

143

understood. When your thought is not understood and dealt with, you struggle, you condemn, you blame, and then you try to force your attention upon a particular idea in opposition to your conditioning, thereby creating further conflict. Don't you see that your thinking is caught up in a useless struggle which can never be creative?"

I was now getting a clearer picture, and Tsang said: "Master, I am grateful for these last few words alone."

Then my friend continued: "When an idea rules your mind you should know what it is and not struggle with it. All ideas are the result of something else, and you should understand their value. When you do this, then there is no struggle, no fear, no limitation, no confusion.

"Your mind is of value only when there is no conflict, no strain, no struggle; when these cease to be, there is peace, and this is the mind I want you to have for our work," he said looking at me.

"You must be alert every moment," he added. "This should be cultivated in your everyday life, not merely at times for specific analysis, but to be aware always in the present; then you will know what is happening. This will develop an understanding of the self, and selfknowledge is the gateway to Wisdom and Truth."

Then he pointed to the Abbot. "He is trying to be spiritual and is stranded through the struggle between good and evil. He imitates and is caught up in the conflict between right and wrong."

"I thought to myself: "That is one for you, Abbot." But my friend did not stop there, for he said: "The Abbot thinks he can find the happy medium, a balance between good and evil. He thinks that God is exercising this balance, so he prays, chants, imitates, conforms and is bound up in his superstition. If he would only discern the false he would know what is true. But his craving to be spiritual means only frustration, sorrow and conflict."

I looked at the Abbot but he did not say anything.

"Good and evil," my friend went on, "grow on the same tree. They have the same root and that is in man's mind only, where it is made up and has no foundation in Truth."

Tsang whispered into my ear: "The Abbot is getting a lecture now."

My friend must have heard him or have read his thoughts for he gently said: "So are you, Tsang!"

"Truth," my friend added, "knows nothing of good or evil, past or future. Truth is the living expression of Life *now,* moment to moment, in which there is no separation, no death, being Eternal and Ever-present. In this ecstasy there is Infinite Love and Wisdom. Your actions will then be in accordance with your living in the present always, and the rewards for such actions are phenomenal."

"Now, my son," and he turned to me, "with this serenity there is the joy of living, there is no need of control or analysis, because you are aware every moment. Thus you are free from all the virtues you think you should have or not have, which fills you with conflict through strain and fear. When you are free of all that bundle of virtues, then there is no fear, no opposites, no confusion, no conflict; there is just Love and Wisdom. For in Reality that is all there is; then you will be truly creative and a channel through which the Master can speak again.

'If you are continually occupied with the self, trying to become, there is always a struggle, but when you know yourself to Be *now,* the struggle ceases; then only can the Life that is free be realised.

145

Your thought and work have been limited by your lack of understanding of your true Being *Now,* not in some distant future."

He went on to explain: "To understand that which is limitless, unconditioned, your mind must not be burdened by the thoughts of the self. The self which is nothing must dissolve away, so that Reality can express Itself in the *Now.* 'I of my own self am nothing."

I was feeling a deep transformation taking place within me. Things that used to trouble me had no place in me now, and I said so.

"I am glad, my son." he said, and he continued: "When your mind was burdened with the conflict of ethics you could not realise the truth of your Being, but now that your mind is no longer bound by ethics, by virtues, by distinctions, by separation, by division, you will comprehend what I mean by spontaneous action, free from reaction, free from time, free from separateness and free from opposites; now the flow of Life performs its own work. In the words of the Master, 'It is the Father who ever abideth in Me, He does the work.'

"Your word then shall not return to you void but will accomplish that which is sent forth to do."

He then looked at the Abbot and said: "Look at the Abbot here, just like your bishops spinning words which are as impotent as the seat he is sitting on."

This startled the Abbot, who said: "I do not believe in all our paraphernalia, master."

"Then why don't you come out of it, Abbot? and be a real helper to mankind."

Chapter VIII

The Abbot hung his head and my friend said: "Many are called but few are chosen!"

"In Reality," he said to the Abbot, "there is only the present; there is no past or future; therefore this understanding cannot be postponed. Free yourself from false virtues and you will be enlightened. This requires the discernment now of your thoughts, your motives, your reactions to what I am saying to you now. Then you will see that ignorance is not the absence of learning but the confusion and conflict of values.

"Are you confused, Abbot? Wondering what is right or wrong? Then you are caught up in the conflict of ideas in your mind. You are an imitator, Abbot; you are trying to mould yourself after a pattern and you have created an image of what you think Reality should be, and you are carefully fashioning yourself after it, thereby losing the substance---Reality Itself. By your imitation how can you realise the enduring happiness of the Ever-present Life? Life is Ever-present, not separate. Truth is unbounded unity. You cannot understand this while your mind is occupied with form, ritual, distinction, division. Only by seeing the false now, Abbot, can you see the true.

"It is because you are inwardly poor that you set up an authority and worship it. You want to lean on someone because you feel you yourself are unequal to the task. You want to shelter in the comfort of an idea that is not Reality, Abbot! Your idea is but an illusion.

"You are binding these lamas just as you yourself are bound hand and foot."

Then he turned to me and said: "Life is Real, It is complete in Itself, expressing Itself freely when you yourself becoming nothing. The self lives in separation, you see yourself separate from others; that is but an illusion, for there is but "One" Life in which there is no division. Thus, you see division is an illusion of the mind, my son.

"You are no longer agitated by the worshiping of virtues or the horror of sin, nor will you follow the narrow path of ethics which prevents understanding.

"You see, the Abbot here has moulded himself after a pattern and he is afraid. To be devoid of fear you must know yourself to Be "Now," understanding your vanities, your jealousies, your envies, your cravings, your longings, your hopes, your regrets and fears. All these disappear when you seek understanding, free from the illusion of *Time*.

"When your mind is full of the false you must empty it through discerning the falseness of it all. Then the mind will become empty of the false, and the Life that is Ever-present will then fill it with its ever-expanding consciousness, which will always be the Reality, while all that is external to Itself will be discerned with wisdom, love and understanding." He was still looking at me as he went on: The One Infinite Life is expressing Itself in Love and Wisdom; only when you limit Its action through narrow, bigoted beliefs do you prevent Its freedom in your own life here and now.

It will be your work, my son, to help free man from the curse of separation, so that the specific Life flowing from the Supreme Fountain of Life Itself through the majestic Angels of the Sun-world can assert Its presence through man, thereby freeing man from his own selfcreated misery. This Life is charged with wisdom and love, knowledge and compassion, heralding in the new age of man's understanding---'MAN' whom the Father 'Consecrated' and sent into the world, He is the Son of God."

With this he ended the day's lesson. We rose and went into a large room set aside for us. The four of us sat down to eat.

Chapter VIII

The Abbot spoke first. He said, "Master, I am willing to do your bidding. Whatever you ask of me I will do."

Then said my friend: "Teach those whom God has placed in your hands the Truth, and you will be the first to rid this country of the superstition that is keeping it in ignorance, slavery and poverty."

The Abbot then rose and went over to where the Master was sitting and said: "Give me your blessing that I may be able for the task before me."

Years later I heard that Ok Valley Monastery had become the most enlightened monastery in the whole of Tibet; even the great seat of Ganden could not compare with it.

Lamas from near and far came to hear the great Abbot of Ok and witness the wonders that he performed.

The remainder of the day was spent in watching some of the lamas practising archery.

Teams from all the monasteries went to Lhasa once a year to compete. This was a great event, and the lamas at Ok were practising for it. The accuracy with which the lamas hit the target was phenomenal. Judgment was the main requirement. A target would be placed over a rise, the archers would have to look at the target, then walk back so many paces until the target was out of sight and by judgment they would shoot the arrows, and seldom did they miss the target.

These teams were at it every day, and the best teams would be picked out of those practising. There were over a hundred archers, and marks were tabulated so that only the very best would be included in the forthcoming competition at Lhasa.

Chapter VIII

When I was a boy I used to shoot rabbits with my bow and arrow on my father's estate, and though I had not practised archery for many years I felt eager to try my skill, so I asked if I could have a try. I was made very welcome by the lamas. In fact, I did very well on the sighted target, but for those out of sight I had many misses. Yet if one had sufficient practice in this judgment one could become proficient. Anyway, I was given a place in one of the teams and there was great fun. Whether it was luck or not, my team won that afternoon and I did more than the average, which made me a bit of a hero. The Abbot was delighted; he really was a delightful fellow and was grateful to have been allowed to listen to the talks we had.

For the next two days I was left to myself to get my mind free from the many different ideas and beliefs. I found now that only facts remained, even a belief in a fact had no place in my mind, so thoroughly did my friend "clean" me out.

My mind was now ready for its first try-out.

I was given a piece of paper on which my friend had written some profound words.

What I had to do was to read these words and then speak about them. No sooner had I started reading them than I felt a charge of electricity had passed through me; my mind went blank for a second, and then I felt a confidence that I never had before. I could feel that I was linked into a fountain of wisdom. I heard myself speaking, I listened and reasoned as the words came, it seemed that I was in two parts, one of which was attached to a fountain of Love, Wisdom and Power; and the other part was feeling and learning at the same time. It was a new and a very strange experience for me.

My friend was pleased indeed.

Chapter VIII

He said: "You will be able to do better yet; gradually you will improve till you can be overshadowed by the great spiritual Being, and the spiritual light will be seen around you as He overshadows you. When that is accomplished you will go back after a few more months into the world from which you came. You will be the same to those who knew you, but there will be a difference which they cannot define.

"While you are working in the world among the people, there will still be taking place a building-up of your inner sheaths so that more and more spiritual power can be used, and being among the people of the world is the best field where this can be done satisfactorily."

From then on I knew I was not alone, and I could tell what influence was with me, St. Anthony the Great of Alexandria was one to whom I had spoken many times through different mediums, but no medium ever became nearly so good as Tsang Tapa. No only could the entities speak but they could do so in their own language, for instance German, French, Italian, Chinese, Hindustani, English, Tibetan, all with perfect ease.

Here was a mechanism that could be used by any entity, no matter of what nationality, sometimes changing over from one language to another without as much as a hesitation.

I enjoyed every minute of the time I stayed in Ok Valley. We worked, we laughed, and I made rapid progress. The Abbot was getting on slowly with his new outlook on Life and religion, but he could not do very much at first, otherwise he would be thrown out by the higher officials at Lhasa---just as the head of the Church would throw out a bishop who tried to break down the idea of the power of sin, of hell and the devil, which kept the people in fear. As long as people were kept in fear they could be controlled and cajoled, for the Church thrived on sin. But as soon as the cause fear is removed there is no more controlling or cajoling.

Often in my own work in the world I have had patients filled with fear through religious bigotry.

I would say: "God is Infinite in nature?" in a sort of inquiring way.

"Oh yes, God is Infinite in nature!" (That was my first leg-in.)

"There cannot be anything outside Him, otherwise He could not be Infinite?"

"Quite correct!" would be the answer.

"And to be infinite He must be everywhere, otherwise He could not be Infinite?"

"That is true."

"So there could be none other but Him?"

"That is so!"

"Well," I said, "that being so, God must be the Devil and Hell must be in Him too. If God is, then the Devil is not. It is the very non-existence of the Devil that makes up the Devil, for there cannot be God and the Devil, God being Infinite in nature. It is like mathematics, the mistake disappears when it is found out, and so does the Devil disappear when he is found out." Shock No.1. Recovery slow!

"But it says in the Bible that there is a Hell and the Devil," I would be told.

"Yes, that is true," I would reply, "but Jesus said: 'Ye read the Scriptures, then think ye found Eternal Life, ye make a mistake.' Then he said: 'Resist not evil,' do not give it a power it does not possess. The Devil is the self and Hell is the mess the self makes. You have only a belief, and idea, which is made up in your mind, but you are afraid to reason it out because you are caught up in your belief. Not until you know what a belief is, can you see how false it is."

"But what about the words of Jesus?" a patient asks.

I reply: "Jesus never wrote any words about the Truth; he knew he could not. He asked

Pontius Pilate: "What is Truth?" Pontius Pilate could not answer Him. In fact he never wrote any words at all. He knew that his words could not reveal the Truth, they could give you an idea of the Truth, and that is *not* the Truth! Men wrote the Bible, men also wrote the New Testament many years after Jesus was crucified and it has been altered a dozen times since by men. You take the word to be Truth when it is not the Truth.

The Truth cannot be found in any book, and not until you know what a word is, will you know that it is not the Truth.

"But Jesus said: 'Get ye behind me, Satan.'"

"So did I," I would reply, "when I found out what Jesus found out in the wilderness.

When I discerned all that was in my mind I knew what the self was. The self was the devil that was hiding the Real. The self was always in front, that is the way of the self, yet the self had no existence; the self existed only because I was ignorant of my Being. This self was the devil that was preventing the expression of the Real, so I said too, 'Get ye behind me, Satan! You are a cheat, you

153

are cheating me out of my true birthright as a Son of God.' When I knew that God was the only One and there was none other but Him, then I knew that I was His Son, not born of the blood or the will of the flesh or the will of man, but of God who is Eternal and Everpresent,

I was free, then the Father performed His own deeds.

"I knew I was, because God is. But I do not know what He is and we are One and can never be separated. The self is a belief in separation, but separation is an illusion. This is the devil and hell or the mess the self makes, because the self only knows separation and seeks only for the self.

"What you have is but an idea in the mind accepted from someone else. You are an imitator because you accept what another says. You are worshipping an idea which is an illusion of the mind. This is not God, for God is neither an idea nor an image, neither an illusion nor a belief. You imitate because you do not know yourself with all your fears and illusions. You do not know what is true because you do not know what is false, so the blind lead the blind and they all fall into the ditch.

"Now, if you were shown what was false you would find out what was true by yourself. Remember, nobody can tell you what Truth is, but you alone can experience Truth when you know what is false. You cannot experience Truth if you accept what another man says, and thus not think for yourself. Those who tell you what Truth is are the false prophets, but you do not know that yet, because you are caught up in your belief.

"You have only to look into your mind to see what is there and you will see it is not the Truth, but merely an idea of the Truth. 'I AM' the Truth. I cannot be anything else, because there is no other Life but the 'One,' in which there is no division; therefore the illusion is in your mind, a self-created illusion, and that which is created is not the Truth. Only that which is not created is the Truth, and you do not know what It is, but you will know that 'IT IS' when you rid your mind of all that is false.

"So your so-called virtue is humbug; trying to become virtuous is covering up what you are. Merely to have an idea of what you are not, that is not virtue. Virtue is an understanding of what you are, without distinction. So-called virture is illusion and bondage. If you do not know what you are, striving to become virtuous will not make you virtuous. Virtue can be found only in understanding what you are. Virtue is freedom, immediate release through understanding what you are. Virtue is seeing what is preventing the expression of Reality.

"Kindness, affection, mercy, generousity, forgiveness are all true expressions of Reality, and this is virtue. This is the only way we can solve our problems, but your so-called virtue cannot solve any problem. Then there is no virtue in becoming virtuous, because virtue exists only in 'Being' *Now*. Virtue is not a matter of time. If you do not know what you are, you have no virtue in you."

Every time I got the opportunity to speak in this way I did so, and I found that the patients always came back for more and more. It paid big dividends because it released the tension of trying "to become," which led only to frustration through living in opposites.

CHAPTER IX

We continued our work day after day until my mind was as clear as crystal. Each day the power grew stronger. The air was crisp and clear, and no inharmonious thought or feeling ever arose between us. We worked every day until we felt slightly tired but not over-tired, for that would retard progress.

Eventually I reached the stage where I could work by myself, which was essential before my training ended.

A meeting had been arranged by Geshi Rimpoche, unknown to me, and he arrived with Dar Tsang from Yangtang, Geshi Malapa from Gonsaka, and Geshi Tung La from Takohu. So there were eight of us now, and with such a company anything could happen.

I saw Geshi Rimpoche speaking to Tsang Tapa (the oracle, which means medium), and I anticipated that we were to have a real seance that night. In fact it had been previously arranged, but this was kept as a surprise for me. I could, however, now read their minds as easily as if they were speaking. I had become expert, thanks to the practice I had during these months of intensive training.

Supper was prepared for us specially in the Abbot's quarters, which were quite large, consisting of a big oblong room with a long table, around which his students sat. This formed a perfect dining-table. There was a general animated conversation, some of it in Tibetan, some in Hindustani, some in English. With English and Hindustani I was quite familiar, and I could make out a good bit of Tibetan now, the Abbot having given me lessons whenever possible. He was a wonderful teacher and knew all the easy ways of putting the words together. Tibetans use as many words as possible with great flourish. When they did this I resorted to reading their minds and that is fatal if you want to learn a language, because to learn a language you must think in that language and not try to read the mind. To read the mind you do not listen to the word otherwise your mental reception becomes distorted, and mind-reading is then impossible.

There was a silence in the animated conversation when my friend spoke in no uncertain terms, condemning the so-called religious hermits of the present time.

He said: "The hermits of to-day have degenerated into a useless, deluded devotees because of the fact that the true teachings of Gautama and Malarepa are no longer understood by the lamas. They are brought up on ritual and know nothing of the inner powers of man.

"At one time suitable candidates were chosen by the great Masters and after a period of training they retired, away from the haunts of men to attain self-enlightenment and to develop the power of the Tibetan Yogi. But what have we to-day? Devotees without any knowledge of the science of Yoga.

"These lamas go into solitude only to waste their lives in this stupid deterioration of the mind and body. They gain nothing by it. Their retirement has become merely a part of their religious ritual."

I asked: "What do they do?"

"Well," he replied, "in the training of the lama he is supposed to spend part of his life in confinement, but without training it is pure folly. The period is three days or three months or three years, generally.

"At first they may retire for three days, then they may retire for three months or three years. They may emerge once more before going in for Life in one of the cells that you see on the mountainside, and once they are locked in a cell they are in complete darkness, their minds being dark as well. On one side of

158

the cell there is a small drain covered with a slate which they use for their daily excretions. On the other side of the cell there is a stone that can be removed from the outside only, through which a daily supply of tea and tsampa is pushed on to a ledge on the inside, and the hand that appears to take in the food must be gloved, for no light must strike any part of the body.

"Many of these deluded devotees go out of their minds before their lifelong confinement comes to an end. They become mental and physical wrecks. They have no training, nor do they know anything about the arts of the Tibetan Yogi. Their lives are a complete waste, with nothing gained."

"But," I ventured to point out, "there are some ascetics who retire into the mountain or into a solitary place and there develop their gifts."

"Certainly," he said, "but they have been trained by a Master Yogi in the first place.

Those who come out of the monastery with only a knowledge of ritual are a debased type, capable only of the physical part of the hermit's life. They prostitute the practice of the adept and are therefore incapable of developing their Spiritual gifts."

Geshi Rimpoche then spoke. I could see that he had gone into that subjective state with his eyes closed, and the timbre of his voice was fascinating to listen to.

"Friends," he said, "I do not decry religion nor the search for Reality, but organized dogma with its rituals, reciting prayers, repeating mantrims, quoting the Gita or the Bible, that is not religion. By calling yourself a lama, a Buddhist, a Christian, a Hindu, or following a ritual, can you find Truth? I think not! In these separate influences you are caught up in the net of organised beliefs, they are the drugs that dull the mind, they offer an escape, thus making the mind dull and ineffective."

No one said a word, because everyone knew that when Geshi Rimpoche spoke like this it was the wisdom of the gods.

"You are caught up," he went on, "in a whole system of authorities, priests and 'gurus'. You do not understand yourself, so you are merely accepting, not inquiring. Because your great grandfather did some ritual and your mother would cry if you don't, is humbug. It is because you are dependent that you are fearful, incapable of finding out what is false---and when you do not know what is false you cannot know what is true.

"You may talk about God and repeat His name a thousand times, but this will not reveal the Truth. The Truth will be hidden from you because you will be folded up in your own prejudices, your own fears. The ignorance of man himself is responsible for this organized religion, whether it be of the East or the West. It is because man is confused that he wants an authority."

No one spoke. Geshi Rimpoche was leading up to something important.

"So having created the authority," he continued, "whether political or religious, you follow its direction in the hope of finding the Truth.

"What you know of Reality through the authority of another is not Truth, and thus you do not know. Since Reality is unknown, how can you seek it through an authority? When you seek an authority you have lost confidence in yourself because you are merely an imitator. It is because you have lost confidence that you create leaders. You read all the holy books you can find. You pursue different ideas which create contradiction, the more imitative you are the less confidence you have in youself, and you merely make your life into a copybook."

I knew this was a lesson for me as well as for the Abbot in fact all of us would benefit by it.

"From childhood," he went on, "you have been told what to read and what to do. You were not allowed to think for yourself. To find out the cause of your confusion you must have confidence in yourself, you must have a deep inward certainty of what is false and what is true.

But you do not know because you have never inquired how you acquired your beliefs or ideas.

"Being confused, do you think that you can find the Truth by reading the Upanishads, the Gita, the Bible or any other book? Do you think you are capable of reading the Truth of it when you yourself are confused? You will merely translate what you read according to your confusion, your likes, your dislikes, your prejudices, your conditioning.

"The Truth is revealed when you understand yourself, your prejudices, your ideas, your beliefs. Truth comes to you; you do not have to go to the Truth. Truth is! You do not create It.

"When you think you are going to the Truth it is merely a projection of your own conditioning. Then it becomes a process of self-hypnosis which is organised religion and there can be *no* conclusion regarding the Truth.

"When you have freed yourself from all your mental formulations you will find that which is *not* a mental formulation. The mind must cease to formulate before you can find the Real. Then you will not belong to any organised religion, neither will you condemn nor criticise, nor will you become an athiest, for that is only another form of belief.

"To find that which is the Real Self you must not make an idea of It, nor can It be separated from Itself in others, because there is no division in Reality. Only by understanding the personal self that is hiding the Real will the false fall away. Then the glory of God, His Love, Wisdom and Power will manifest, for it is ever-present and eternal and you do not create It."

He opened his eyes again. He looked at me and then at the Abbot.

"Seek not after power for what it will give you, otherwise you will lose the Real. When you have the Real you have everything. You do not develop the Real, *the Real will develop you.* Therefore, *Be Now!* For you are Real only in the Now, not in the past nor in the future.

If you are not Real Now, then you will never be, because only in the Now is the Real expressed."

No one spoke after this. There was silence for at least five minutes.

The moon was rising; it was full, coming up behind the mountain. It had a reddish glow, and as it rose higher it became pure silver, white and clear. The shadows of the mountains were now in the valley below, while the peak of Chomolhari was reflecting the silvery light from the moon. It was a perfect scene in a perfect night, the air still, crisp and clear. It was as if the Masters of old were around and about us. The feeling was one of excited expectancy. Then Geshi Rimpoche broke the silence as he said: "We now have the perfect circle, the purest atmosphere to create the necessary conditions for our friends to visit us this evening.

Chapter IX

We have all gathered together before in my own sanctum except that my son and the Abbot were not with us then, but now we have the perfect combination to make our circle complete for materialisations to-night. It is a delight to have our friends come to speak to us in their own voices."

Turning to me he said: "You will experience the fact that there is no death and it will no longer be a belief but a fact. Not that we need a demonstration to convince us that there is no death, but we enjoy the company of our friends just as naturally as you would your friends on earth. Not only will there be those who have passed on from the flesh but also those who are still in the flesh will come. This, "turning to me again, "will be a new experience for you, my son."

I said: "Not quite, for I have seen you before beside me."

"Yes, that is correct, but to see and speak to our other friends just as I am speaking to you will be an experience you have not yet had."

"That is true, and it will be wonderful!" I exclaimed. I was eager to begin.

The door of the Abbot's room led out on to the balcony and faced down the valley.

Geshi Rimpoche opened the door.

I said: "But do you not need darkness for materialisation?"

"Oh no," he replied, "we do not need darkness; in the light of the moon you will see as clearly as you would in daylight."

I remarked: "In the West they need darkness for a materialisation."

"Yes," he said, "but they do not have the perfect combination, and their methods are clumsy and unsatisfactory."

I did not say any more, because I realised that the power that I had already seen demonstrated was beyond the comprehension of the ordinary mind, and there was no reason why there should not be something that I did not yet understand.

In any event, Geshi Rimpoche showed that he had experience, for he set about the arrangements with a confident understanding of what he was doing. First, he ordered the table to be put to the side, out of the way. Then he arranged us in the way that he wanted. He said: "To get the best results I want an uninterrupted flow of the magnetic force so as to build up the ectoplasm. Those who are still on or near the earth can show themselves with comparative ease, but those who have left the earth-influence need a substance in which the vibration of their etheral bodies can be reduced so that they can be seen and heard with our physical eyes and ears."

So he sat us as follows: I on his right; on his left he put the Abbot, and opposite him sat my friend, on the right of my friend he place Dar Tsang, and on the left Malapa; then came Tung La, and opposite Tung La sat Tsang Tapa.

Then he said: "You understand that at the four points of the 'plan' are the positive," and he drew on the floor with a piece of chalk as follows:

Myself Geshi Rimpoche Abbot

O + O

Tung La + + Tsang Tapa

O + O

Chapter IX

Malapa My Friend Dar Tsang

At the points so marked he drew a +; then he drew a circle in-between each segment, linking them all up; and from the centre he drew another four lines ending with the a small circle.

"Now," he explained, "the + represents the positive element, and the circle represents the negative element , just like the two poles of electricity, if the one is without the other no relative force is created."

He went on: "Electricity is in the atmosphere and all around us; it is in its nebulous form, but it becomes active in the relative world when the two elements unite."

Then he filled in the centre. "This is the mixing bowl,' he said, "in which the ectoplasm is formed; then it will spread out enveloping the whole room, going as far as the door, the walls of the room keeping it as it were together."

"Now," he said, "when we are ready to begin, the chemists in the etheral world will come and they will use their own formula in regulating the density of the ectoplasm for the materialisations.

"The gross form of this substance comes from us from our magnetic body, It is crude and thick and often unusable, but when it is regulated by the etheral chemists into its perfect texture those around us here, unseen at the moment will be seen and heard."

"Of course," he said, "there is much more to it than what I have said. It is a science that is not yet really understood; although your scientists are delving into the structure of matter, they have not yet grasped the fact that the electro-magnetic force is behind all form, and, in fact, all the atomic structure of the Universe. It is the slowing of the electro-magnetic force that makes the different textures of matter from the very highest ethereal down to the grossest physical, and there is no division; you cannot tell where one ends and the other begins; it is one complete indivisible substance.

"If I may give you an example, a crude one for lack of a better, take a piece of solid pitch, add heat to it, and it gradually begins to lose its solidity. The gradual dissolving process begins from the solid mass until it becomes a liquid; you cannot see a division from the time of its solidity to the state of its fluidity. Keep on applying more heat until it reaches its gaseous state, and from the solid mass into its invisible form you cannot detect any division.

"From the visible to the invisible and beyond, there is no division, and from beyond the invisible to the visible there is no separation , and in and through, supporting this change, is the changeless basic substance that remains stable always. And beyond and within is the Creativeness that uses this substance to create form. The form changes back into the original basic substance, which remains stable. This is called creation and disintegration; they are one, and not separate forces."

"Now, what we do not know is the Uncreated which alone is creative. And," he continued, "this Uncreated is within you; you can discern all that is relative to It, but you cannot discern what It is itself because it will always be discerning that which is external to Itself.

"You cannot tell what your consciousness is---try to see if you can, and you will find that consciousness is always discerning what is relative to itself. It cannot turn back upon itself.

But when all the relative is understood and known, then the Unknown can be experienced. It cannot be known, for the known cannot know the Unknown; therefore the known is not the Real, the Real is the Unknown, the Unknowable. But when you have reached the point where one merges into the other, there is awareness and creativeness at point; the totality of Creativeness is behind point, and point is where It is expressed through you, and then that which is the Real manifests. *This is the Master*! He is the point through which the Whole works. Jesus said: "It is the Father who ever abideth within Me, He is performing His own deeds."

Then he looked at me, and continued:"Therefore, the proof is when you have reached creativeness. At that point you become aware of all that is relative and therefore you know that it is not creative; the Creative is the Uncreated in you and me, the All of Creativeness is behind point.

"Now what we will witness here to-night is phenomenon. It is interesting and instructive; it is the nearest to that religion which will make us realise that we are all One, the Fatherhood of God and the brotherhood of man. Man's belief of separation, his belief in authority, his following of an authority, his selfishness, his cravings for Spiritual and material gain, all these will pass when this Truth is universally known.

He then directed: "Concentrate on the centre, and you will see the ectoplasm forming."

Sure enough, there it was, forming into a white cloud. The light from the moon showed it up clearly. It began to whirl above our heads as well. We seemed to be enveloped in it. It eventualy filled the whole room and the doorway like a white cloud. In fact it was as if we were enveloped in the clouds---such was the feeling I got. I felt I was transported from the earth into the clouds and that soon we would be talking to the Masters of old and to relatives who had passed from their earthly abode; and some who were still in the flesh would also come to talk to us.

Chapter IX

Words fail to describe the whole wonderful demonstration. The great Malarepa was the first to speak. He spoke to us in three languages, Tibetan, Hindu and English.

He said: "I have come to give you further enlightenment. The occult power you try to possess is not the Real. The Real is beyond and is so magnificent that what I say can only create ideas about It. Yes It is far beyond what the mind can make up in regard to It. There is so much rubbish and nonsense taught and all this blinds you to the Truth. For instance, reincarnation as you believe, is nowhere near the Truth.

"You believe that the late Dalai Lama is reincarnated in the present Dalai Lama. This is not fact. If the great Buddha were incarnated he would be free from ritual and the nonsense you carry on with. His great wisdom would be shown in his acts. But what do you find? A mere child in wisdom and understanding! Reincarnation as stated in your religion is but humbug and is holding everyone in subjection to a superstition of fear and ignorance.

"I tell you, 'Truth' is not in any way like what is being taught. What is being taught is an absolute fabrication of the Truth. The man you called the last Dalai Lama is not in the body of the present Dalai Lama as your religion teaches. I want you to see that it is merely a belief and not a fact, certainly not the Truth.

"There is reincarnation, but not as you understand it. The Spirit of the one God---the Life---is in the present Dalai Lama as it was in each preceding Dalai Lama, but the present Dalai Lama is not aware of this Truth. It is the one Spirit that is in each and everyone, and only when this is realised through knowing what is false does the wisdom and power of the Spirit manifest.

"I urge you to lead the people away from this stupid nonsense that creates selfhypnosis.

Chapter IX

I am speaking to you in modern language so that you can understand what I say."

He spoke for a long time to Geshi Rimpoche, and I heard him say: "Care must be excercised so that you do not hinder the work to come, for many are not yet ready to understand that Life is not separated by so-called death. There is but one Life and this Life is Eternal. More will come after me to speak to you. Your friend the Hermit of Ling-Shi-La is here to-night."

Malarepa seemed to be the conductor in the astral, and Geshi Rimpoche conducted on the physical.

Still they came, many of them, and as they reached the door they became visible. It was a wonderful sight, a wonderful experience. I never saw anything like it before or since.

About an hour or so later, St. Anthony of Alexandria and Paul the Apostle came direct to me, and I will relate what St. Anthony said later in this chapter. But I want to tell you first what convinced me that all this was real and not the figment of my imagination.

My mother came to me. I could see her form and face as well as I did when she was on earth, except that she was young-looking and wonderfully radiant. She spoke to me in Gaelic to prove that it was she.

"It is truly me, your mother; your father is with me, and so is your friend John Sutherland."

She said: "I am very happy because of the work you are doing, and we are all helping."

Her face shone bright and beautiful when she said that, as if the feeling gave her great joy.

There were six hours of this, coming and going, and the details alone would fill another volume. Many who were still in the physical came, including the great hermit of Ling-Shi-La, of whom Geshi Rimpoche had told me.

The hermit said to me: "You are coming to stay with me at my hermitage."

Geshi Rimpoche had not told me this, but it happened that I did go to stay at the hermitage, and of this I will tell you in another chapter.

Then, near the end, there was the most brilliant light; it shone all over the room. It lit up everything as if the sun was shining. So bright was this light that we had to close our eyes at first; then we gradually became accustomed to it, and in this light appeared the Master himself.

He came to give His blessing.

Those of you who have read my book *Divine Healing of Mind and Body* (The Master speaks again) will realise the truth of what I say; it was the culmination of all my training in the Himalayas.

This indeed was the most remarkable seance I had ever seen, and I will probably never see the like again.

I knew then that there was no separation between the material and the Spiritual, what separated us was but a veil of ignorance. But enlightenment was coming into the world, and soon all the darkness of the mind would disappear and those with spiritual gifts would no longer be persecuted.

A new religion is coming into the world, not a sectarian religion or a dogma or a creed, but one that will reveal that death is but the doorway into a higher state of the one Life that is eternal and ever-present, showing that there is no division between us and those who have gone on. The Masters of old, even Jesus, are one with us, as he said he would be, even unto the end of the world.

Words cannot describe the beauty and the glory of such a wonderful revelation.

The science of the various arts was discussed. St. Anthony spoke to me especially about healing. He was the great therapeutist of ancient Egypt, and healing was his great subject, that is why, as he said, he was detailed by greater ones than himself to help me in my work along with many others who also were working and would continue to do so when I go back again into the world I came from.

The discourse on healing was specially directed to me. The others who came talked to those present about various things.

Apparently the whole seance was conducted in a perfect way. No one was allowed to "chip in "while another talked to one in particular, though ten or more were in the room at the same time.

I was keenly interested in what St. Anthony had to say to me. I had spoken to him before but not in such a complete way.

He said: "God is glorified through the Son of Man." I knew the meaning of those words, for he had spoken of them to me before. Then he continued speaking to me personally as though there were no one else in the room.

He said: "Since time began, men and women have been given the power to heal and to teach. Some of the healings have been so amazing that the mind of man could not comprehend them. Thus sceptics arose, and made every effort to deny these transformations on the grounds of their apparent impossibility."

"Divine Healing," he went on, "has achieved wonders where all other methods have failed, yet man does not realise the mighty power of the Spirit, because the mind cannot penetrate the realm which is beyond it. The mind can reason only on what it knows, but that which it does not know, that which is beyond reason, cannot be defined, and it is in this realm that Divine Healing takes place."

"Yes," I remarked, "many have wondered how Divine Healing takes place, how that which is unseen could accomplish such a complete and instantaneous change, and they still want to reduce it into terms which would merely give the mind an idea and not the Truth."

Then St. Anthony spoke again: "Phenomena of any kind are produced through a law that is intelligent, otherwise there would be no phenomena.

For instance, if you have a fear of anything or you have faith in anything, there is an intelligence that operates in both what you think in fear and think in faith and produces exactly according to how you think in fear and in faith, that is the law of thought-action or electro-magnetic activity for in fact the body is electrical, being composed of atoms of energy.

"But Truth is like mathematics; It is exact. When an error is discovered and corrected, it disappears. You cannot tell me why two and two make four and not five, you cannot investigate mathematics, just as you cannot investigate Truth. You can investigate only error.

Truth, like mathematics, is eternally true and ever-present and is not subject to change, therefore not subject to error. That is why Divine Healing is so perfect.

"You can investigate the laws operating around you, but even these come from That which is beyond the mind of man which cannot be investigated.

"The cause of the chaos that surrounds you is that man has failed to understand the underlying principle of Life. This stupidity has prevented the best brains from understanding the Law of Life operating in man himself.

"To deny the existence of the law of mathematics would be stupid; so is denying the existence of the Law of Truth. You can understand the Law of Truth, but you cannot tell what Truth is, only that It is, just as mathematics is. You can work with Truth just as you can with mathematics. There is a true note in music which is harmonious; there is no such thing as a false note, there is only a noise, and that is not harmony.

"To deny, does not help. To deny the false is to give it recognition, a reality that it does not possess. But to understand how it arises, then you will see how false it is. Then you will see that the false is created by the self which has no existence in the Real. The Real which is harmony comes into Being when you see that the false has no existence except in the self.

"The false tries to hang on to the self because that is the only existence the false can ever have; hence the illusion.

"Jesus never claimed any power of his own. He said: 'It is the Father who ever abideth within me, He is performing His own deeds.' Neither did he make something of himself: he said 'Of my own self I am nothing.'

"But when you take upon yourself the cloak of healer and say, 'I am a healer or a prophet' you limit yourself to the personal; that is why so many fail. The self hides the Divine, so you must get the self out of the way; the self is nothing, and the sooner you realise this the better it will be for you and all who come to you.

"Jesus seemed to be an outside agency to those who looked upon him as separate from themselves and God but this was only because they did not know their true Father and therefore they did not know his. Had they known the Father of Jesus to be theirs also, they would have been free. Jesus said that he was nothing by himself, but all was possible with the Father. He knew that he could not be separate from the Life which is yours and mine. Therefore he works through the Cosmic which works through the individual. You must learn to do likewise. It is difficult for those caught up in conformity and separation to realise this Divine Power, but those who have experienced the Divine Power have definite proof of its Reality.

"When I am speaking to you about the Omnipresence my words are relative, and it would seem that I am speaking about something apart from myself. But it is not so. I can speak to you only in relative terms to help you find the Real within yourself."

He continued: "I know that you have already dealt with the relative and understand what I mean. The Master said, "Know ye not I am in the Father and the Father is in me?" This was to show the unity in the Consciousness that is creative in all who understand that He gave them power to become sons of God. 'What I see the Father do, I do likewise.'

"Now you realise that sickness is mostly the effect of certain causes and neglect of natural laws. This comes about through ignorance, through fear, through lack of Love (lack of giving love), lack of understanding the self which is always seeking Love.

"Sickness is the symptom showing that the body and mind has lost its natural rhythm, and the *'struggle'* to regain it is the disease. In other words, if you continue to neglect the natural laws and at the same time continue to struggle with the 'dis-ease', the attention of the mind becomes focused upon the condition because the body is talking back to the mind and the mind is caught up in what the body is feeling. Now, the mind is struggling, making a great effort to save the body. It is this struggle that is causing all the disturbance and displacements of the atoms resulting in pain and discomfort. When this Truth is known the struggle ceases.

"The mind is conscious of feeling, and this feeling is registered in the mind as a disease.

This disease is given a name so that the mind can hold on to it. If the name conveys to the mind an incurable disease the mind may accept it, thus creating a further burden. Only when man sees that the cause is through ignorance of the truth of his Being and through the neglect of the natural laws, does the burden fall away, and then the Spirit-Life transforms the mind and the body responds to Nature's perfect action."

I said: "I can see very clearly that one is conscious of disease by the abnormal condition of the body?"

"Yes," he replied, "when there is a disruption among the cells of the body, a sad report is carried to the brain centres, and then the conscious part of the mind identifies itself with illhealth.

Fear and apprehension enter because the complete power of the Spirit is not realised.

When the mind accepts the Truth of Being, the brain centres are informed; and reconstruction sets in. But when the mind is caught up in the struggle it is not capable of using its first line of defence--- Divine Reason---and accepts the report of the disturbance as final. When the Truth of your Being is realised then the True healing takes place. Sometimes the mind is so charged with the Truth that complete and instantaneous transformation takes place. This is Divine Healing."

So engrossed was I in what he was saying that I took no notice of what was going on around me, and he continued without interruption: "What really happens in sickness is that a consciousness of the Truth of your Being has disappeared from the mind and a consciousness of ill-health has taken control of the mind. There is a loss of cheerfulness, the feeling of vigour has gone.

What fate has befallen the mind that supported the body? The Truth has temporarily gone from the mind that has fallen under the spell of the illusion of the reality of sickness; the mind has surrendered its knowledge of the sovereignty of the Spirit to the forces of disorder and confusion."

And he added: "I am speaking as one who has watched the mind give up its sovereignty."

"Now," he continue, "some resort to drugs as the final agency for recovery, and because this recovery is not forthcoming a further acceptance of the condition is the result. But if by some means a chemical change takes place, there is a change for the better, and this causes further confusion if the trouble returns; and when the patient finds that, in the end, drugs are no longer any help it leads to further depression and apprehension.

"You must realise that the body is not an exclusive combination of chemical reactions; it is endowed with an Intelligence, a knowing-how, an amazing organisation for the maintenance of bodily functions. This is the animating power of Life which is fundamental in producing motion and transformation.

"Natural remedies, such as herbs, biochemics, homeopathy, hydrotherapy, have in many cases acted upon the cell structure and produced a chemical reaction. This produces a powerful suggestion on which the mind is induced to act. Such action on the mind will being to reproduce a consciousness of health and restoration of the balance and harmony within the body. But if the mind is left in this state alone, without understanding the laws of the inherent power of the Spirit within, the second state may be worse than the first."

"You see," he said, "it is the self that is caught up in disease. It is the self that knows disease. The Spirit knows nothing of disease. It is the self that is selfish, ingathering, acquisitive, hateful, antagonistic, unforgiving and violent, and this is the cause of most sickness.

"The Impersonal Spirit knows nothing of these things, hence the Impersonal is Healing.

The more impersonal you become, the more loving and kind you become, because the Impersonal is Love, and Love is healing. Love is God and God is Love and the foundations of all perfect action in which there is no reaction.

"When you see that the personal self is always taken up with the external, with struggle, with war inside and out, then you will understand the cause of the trouble; and, when this is understood, the inner self which is impersonal is freed, then the radio-activity of Life's forces is released.

These electro-magnetic waves of Nature's forces begin to transform the mind and body.

"This inner atomic action creates strong suggestions to the subconscious mechanism which in turn starts instantaneous action throughout the whole mind and body because of the strong currents of energy which are moving in the right direction, sweeping all before it from within outwardly, quelling the existing confusion. The mind and body feel the relief and as the struggle ends, the momentum is kept in the right direction.

"There must be a giving-up of the idea of disease as the confusion and chaos dies down, and when peace is established the body ceases to talk back, and harmony is established.

"Once harmony is established in this way, through understanding, the mind and body is transformed regardless of the nature of the disease or the length of time of the chronic condition.

"With true guidance the patient begins to realise that the suffering is a temporary and artificial thing, and anything that is temporary is transitory and has no foundation of its own. It is the ignorant self which is caught up in things external. The Reality is in no way like the ignorant self. Reality is the Impersonal self which is whole and complete without a flaw."

"If disease were real," he said, *"it could not be healed, since Reality is not subject to change.* The self is born into fear by the aid of suggestions from those who fear. The fear of death is the cause of most suffering in the human family. Then the removal of this fear is of first importance."

"I want you to realise," he emphasised "that there is not a dead particle in the Living Universe. There cannot be a dead part of Life. There is no difference between Life and death; they are one and the same, as you now see. It is but a change from one phase to another in Life Eternal.

"Life continues in its more perfected abode, and the individual consciousness of Life becomes more aware. Therefore you must eliminate the fear of death from the mind so that the consciousness of Eternal Life is established. This is the greatest aid to the healing of mind and body, because the consciousness of fear is destructive to the functions of both, while a consciousness of Life renews their proper function. 'Call no man your father on earth for one is your Father who is Eternal.'

"Perfect healing of mind and body can be done only when the fear of disease and death has disappeared. But you must know yourself before you can help another. Even the dullest mind can be penetrated by an enlightened consciousness."

"Remember," he stressed, "that mantrims are not much help to a mind that is full of fear, for it often intensifies the dominant idea of the trouble; thus you are only creating opposites. You hold an idea of health while struggling with ill-health. You have an idea of Life while struggling with death, an idea of good while struggling with evil, and so on and so on.

"But with skilful, intelligent words through understanding, the patient will become receptive and willing to co-operate, and then a change begins to take place, sometimes instantaneously.

"The power of the Truth of Being sets in motion electro-magnetic vibrations which reach the mind of the patient and begins to break up the negative mental and conditioning that is binding him. By this means the mind of the patient is reached either from a short or long distance. At that very hour the servant was healed. 'Daughter, be of good cheer, they faith hath made thee whole.' These sayings you are familiar with, now see that you realise their true meaning."

He paused for a moment, and then continued: "With the knowledge of the truth of your Being, your aura is purified and your thoughts become dynamic. Realise that everything in Nature is harmless to you and you are harmless to all Nature. When you are not afraid of Nature you can control Nature in the raw, for you have been given power and dominion over all things.

Chapter IX

"See the nothingness of the self, know that you are nobody, and your humility will be the channel through which the Spirit can do Its work. Take the breaks off, God will do the rest.

"Acquire your faith through understanding, and not through the opposite, fear. If it rises from fear then you have no faith, you are caught up in the opposites of fear and faith.

"Develop a willingness to listen; the casting-off of the burden is a great help to the patient.

"Be impersonal by seeing beyond the personal, knowing that the Spirit is not affected by disease or death, good or evil, success or failure.

"Remember at all times that you must first heal yourself before you heal the patient.

What I mean is, to rid your mind of all disturbing elements. By doing this the Divine Power acts without hinderance. Transform all things by the spiritualising power of Love and Wisdom.

Remember that every disturbing influence is like a guerilla, hiding in the corner of the mind, waiting for his comrades to arrive, and when they gather in sufficient numbers they launch an attack on the unsuspecting individual and lay him low.

"These elements thrive in ignorance. The cure is understanding. Spiritualise the patient's consciousness with your own powerful Spiritual light of understanding, so that when his light is lit it shall shine in the darkest corner, thereby lighting up the mind and body with the Light that never dims.

"The world is sick because the individual is sick. Confusion and ignorance are the cause. Remove these two impostors and the Divine man will appear in all his glory as he was made, in the likeness of his Creator.

"The task before you may seem great but our radio waves of Love will go with you.

You will not delay. Go back into the world you know, as soon as you are finished here, and may the Almighty aura of the Christ of God surround you."

Then he took his departure.

I was struck dumb by the wonderful lesson. Only one who knows could have spoken as he did, and I knew it was true. It must have been over half an hour since he began to speak to me, but it seemed like only a moment of time that disappeared into the timeless, for I was in Eternity at that moment.

* * * * * * * *

Now I want to tell you of another fact that made this meeting so real. After my mother spoke to me, my bosom friend Jock Sutherland, who was killed in 1915 in the first World War, spoke. He always called me "Murdo" with a very Highland accent; he came from the Highlands and spoke Gaelic. We had been bosom pals for many years, so we talked about old times and laughed together while he recalled the following story of which only we two knew.

One New Year's Eve, in Glasgow, Jock and I had a few whiskies. Jock was fond of whisky but he could not take very much. That night he became violently sick and began to vomit so badly that he dislocated his jaw. We happened to be passing the Western Infirmary at the time, and I took him in there. The doctor on duty, a friend of mine, was busy. By this time Jock was getting somewhat difficult, he could not even speak.

So I said to him: "Open your mouth, you idiot, I will do this myself." I put my two thumbs on his back molars, gave a quick downward thrust and, click, in went his jaw.

When he told me this there could be no doubting. He had a very prominent forehead and it showed quite clearly. Then he tried to give me some advice but someone shut him up.

When the meeting was over, we sat and talked; everyone seemed to have been rejuvenated. Tea was brought in, and I had still a few boxes of Huntley & Palmer's biscuits left, so we all enjoyed ourselves, talking until daybreak.

As the sun came up we went out to watch it rising from behind the beautiful mountain of Chomolhari. To see the sunrise was apparently a common occurence with the Masters beyond the Himalayas, but to me it was the greatest experience of its kind that I ever had. It put the seal on all that I had seen and learned.

My friend came over and sat down beside me, and he said: "You have a wonderful venerable Spirit friend in St. Anthony."

"Yes," I said, "I know now that I have many wonderful friends and all of them I love very much, including you."

Then he put his arm around my shoulders and said: "It is the Love of God that unites us all together to do His will."

CHAPTER X

Next day I did not feel so tired as I had thought I would be after the all-night sitting. In fact I felt very much wide awake, though we did nothing except just what it pleased us to do. In the afternoon I lay down and began to think of the Hermit of Ling-Shi-La. I closed my eyes and I saw a picturesque, peaceful lake set in green foilage, with trees farther up the mountainside.

Around the lower parts of the mountain were tall rhododendron trees in full bloom, some pink, some white, some crimson. In the centre of the lake was an island, and on this island was a house of unusual and charming design surrounded with shrubs and flowers, the like of which I had never seen before.

Green palm trees were around the green lawn on which the house stood. I wondered to whom such a lovely place belonged when I saw the Hermit of Ling-Shi-La working among the flowers.

I felt someone near me and I opened my eyes, to find my friend by my side. I informed him: "I must have been travelling, for I have seen the most beautiful place secreted on an island in the middle of the lake, with trees and beautiful flowers all around it. As I wondered to whom the place belonged I saw the Hermit himself tending his flowers."

My friend replied: "You have just visited the Hermit. The place you saw is where he lives. It is away over the Tsang Po River in the beyond, country which is still an unexplored region of Tibet. He has the most beautiful place in the world and he attends to it all by himself.

You have just experienced astral travelling, at which the Hermit is an adept. I will tell you the story about him.

Chapter X

"He was an abbot in the Ganden Monastery many years ago, and he taught philosophy and magic. He had been practising astral projection just as you were doing, when he discovered this lovely lake with an island in it. So he set out to find it. After many months he returned and said: "I have found my home at last.' When he told the others where it was they said: 'But no one has ever been able to get into that valley because of the continuous hurricane that blows over the mountain pass; besides, there is no known path into it.'

"He replied: 'I have found a way in, and I shall build my hermitage there. There is no evidence of anyone being there in the physical, and only those who have mastered astral projection can enter, which suits me perfectly. I will now master the art of astral travel completely.' The secret passage into this valley is known only to the Hermit himself; no one yet has ever been there in the physical but himself."

"Well," I told my friend, "the Hermit said I was to stay with him for a while."

"Yes," came the reply, "and then you will truly learn to speak with the gods. I only hope I may have the privilege of coming with you."

Next morning lying on the table beside my couch was a thick parchment giving details about the way to the Hermitage, also advising me what I should take with me. On my friend's table was a similar copy. By some miraculous means these instructions had been apported during the night.

I said to my friend: "This is more mysterious than ever."

He replied: "A material object is very easily transported by those who know how. After certain development, one is able to contact the

Yogi who have passed from the physical and who understand all about apporting. They do this work frequently in Tibet."

I said: "Then it appears that the Hermit can write down instructions and ask these Spirit Yogi to transport them?"

"Oh yes," he replied, "that is easy. You see, they know the secret of materialisation and dematerialisation. You have already heard that matter is but an invisible substance which can be made visible. All is mind---there is no such thing as matter. Matter is a name you have given to something that you see and feel, but the name of a thing is not the thing itself. The name merely becomes an idea in your mind and that is all you know about it. But, you see, the Hermit is a Master Yogi himself, and with the Spirit Yogi, both of them understand vibrations of the various densities of substance that you call matter, can apport an article any distance."

"Now," he went on, "everything being a vibration in mind, and consciousness being the ruling factor, the Hermit consciously knows how to raise the vibration of material substance into its astral vibration and can hold it there, for he has already freed himself from the idea of the solidity of matter. The Yogi work with him and, by their combined efforts, that piece of parchment you seen there with the writing on is raised in vibration, writing and all intact, and is held in that state while being transported through the ether; then it is materialised and you see it before you. There is no magic about it when you know how dematerialisation and materialisation are done."

"Yes," I remarked, "I have seen apporting at a seance of Mr. Bailey's in Sydney. In fact, I still have some of the apports in my possession."

Chapter X

"We shall hear more about it when we see the Hermit," said my friend. "He is considered to be as great as the great Malarepa himself."

"So," I said, "how soon can we start? You know I have not very much time, and time is flying now."

He replied: "We will start to-morrow."

"I am so glad you are coming with me," I confided to him, "I do really think I could not do it without you; besides travelling alone is not much fun, especially in unexplored Tibet."

"I am glad I am coming with you," he assured me. "We will not take much with us; we will travel light, for it is going to be a difficult journey. If it was easy, others would be there. It is, in fact, the most difficult place to reach. That is why the Hermit chose it."

On the following day we started; only the two of us, because of the difficulty in reaching the place and because others would not be welcome to the Sanctuary of Sanctuaries.

We decided to pick up on the way what food we could, and the last part of the journey we left in the lap of the gods.

We struck out towards Gyantse in the early morning. A howling, freezing wind was blowing down the Chomolhari, which was still covered with clouds. The country we were now passing through was barren and stony, yet I could see some yaks feeding, and I wondered what they were eating.

My friend pointed to the way the Everest expeditions take. "But we will keep to the trade route as far as the Gyantse," he said, "and then we will branch to the left till we reach the Tsang Po, the great Brahmaputra at Padong, where we will get a yak hide coracle." (He knows all about it already, I thought.)

Chapter X

We reached a place called Dochen that evening, and we went down to a lake of clear water. Beyond it was a magnificent range of mountains covered with snow. We watched the fish which could be seen clearly in the still water.

"How long will it be still?" I wondered, for any moment a fierce storm might rise.

We fixed our beds for the night and after supper we went out to watch the sun setting.

The reflection in the lake was truly beautiful. The mountain range reflected itself in the calm surface. I took a picture with my small pocket camera and you could not tell the real from the reflection.

I was anxious to hear my friend speak again about the things we both loved so much, and I said:

"If this were America it would be artificialised in twelve months."

"Yes," he replied, "the majority of people know only the objective world, a world which formulates laws, regulations, creeds , and dogmas. They live in a world that is artificial and therefore they know only the artificial, so they want to change Nature also to their standard of existence. They are caught up in their own creations and lose the creativeness of the Uncreated."

He was like Geshi Rimpoche now; he spoke slowly and distinctly, so that I should not miss the meaning of what he said.

"Life remains Itself," he continued, "no matter in what form It is expressing Itself.

When this is understood fully the creativeness becomes a Reality in you. The form is this living Energy in manifestation. Pluck a flower and It is there, and in a handful of earth that you hold in your hand, It is there. Then the world is no longer a prison house, for the air, the sky, reveals Its Living Presence.

"Now, if what I am saying is to be of any value to you, you must experience this in a deeper state of consciousness. It must be a livingness that is not merely a mental formulation. This comes as you clear the mind of all hinderances, and it is done automatically as you see the false; then you will know that a mental formulation is not the Truth, and you will know also that if we make this merely an intellectual discussion you will miss the experience and transformation that must take place within.

"When you see that your mental formulations regarding matter are problematical you will cease to regard solidity as something to be carried, something to stumble over. When you realise that it is the manifestation of the Unmanifest you will free yourself from these mental formulations that limit you. You will know freedom in a free Universe where formerly there was to you nothing but limitations."

He stopped here for a minute, for he knew that an automatic change was taking place in my mind. Then he continued:

"You can reach that state of consciousness that enables the Creative Life to work with effortless spontaneity to achieve the perfection which It Itself is. You will realise that the 'One'

Life is creating within you with effortless perfection as it is manifesting throughout the whole Universe, for there is no separation between the Life in you and me and the Life that is Universal in Its omnipresence, in Its omnipotence and in Its omniscience. Wherever there is perfection, there the Absolute has found release through the mind that has been freed from its own formulations. The Absolute has found release through Its own Creation. Only through your continual awareness can this be done, only through the silent awareness that is active does the Absolute function."

"So you see," he went on, "when the mind is freed from its own formulations, its beliefs, its ideas, there comes a silence beyond time, a silence in which you become conscious of the Reality of your Being. In this freedom there is the releasing of the Creative Energy, with a conscious directive Power that is unknown to the ordinary man. "In great works, in industry, in the arts and crafts, in healing and in oratory, there is the hand of genius when you co-operate in freedom with Life's Creative Intelligence, and all look with amazement on what has been accomplished. This is the Creativeness within, being given free expression through the unconditioned mind. The Unmanifested---the Uncreated---the Absolute is released through the mind that has freed itself from its own conditioning."

He paused for a moment and then went on: "Understand this clearly. Man and not God made yesterday and to-morrow; you will notice that they are but formulations in your mind.

Where is yesterday and where is to-morrow?"

I ventured to say: "I can see now that they exist only in the mind. For God is everpresent in the Now. Yesterday becomes a memory and to-morrow is but a hope; NOW is the only time."

"Splendid!" he exclaimed, "I was waiting for this. Now we can go further."

Then he said: "To live in the ever-present is freedom. For there cannot be any good or evil; no past or future, no success or failure, no health or ill-health. None of these opposites exists in the Presence that is eternally Present. They exist only in the mind that is caught up in opposites and is merely moving backwards and forwards from one to the other."

"Oh," I exclaimed, "I see now why people struggle."

"Yes, and their struggle is a further burden. The Christ, the only begotten Son of the Father, exists in the whole of humanity and does not age or die.

When this is discovered through your awareness moment-to-moment the Eternal Christ is revealed."

"As ye know ME as I am, so shall ye be," I quoted.

"Yes," he said, "the same Christ to-day as was two thousand years ago. 'All power is given unto Me in Heaven and earth.'"

"Now," I could not help saying, "everything has changed; the old ideas of limitation, of hell and the devil and other ideas, all have vanished."

"Yes, that falsehood exists only in the conditioned mind, but when all conditioning is dissolved away we will have the Truth that sets man free. No longer will there be differing creeds, antagonisms, conforming to a ritual or to a pattern, for no longer will there be a pattern to follow. To follow a pattern is to imitate, and imitation is not understanding. Not until man frees himself from his own conditioning can he find the Truth that sets him free."

"Yes," I remarked, "man is still eating of the fruit of the Tree of Knowledge of Good and Evil. Not until he finds out what he is doing will he cling to the Tree of Life, which alone is his salvation."

"Yes, that is so," my friend affirmed, "The Tree of Knowledge of Good and Evil grows out of man's own mind, while the Tree of

Salvation---Life---grows out of God, being eternal and ever-present, and it knows nothing of good and Evil. Yet man is preaching good and evil, hell and the Devil, and so the blind lead the blind.

Man must become aware of his oneness with the Ever-present and not be caught up in a struggle between good and evil, fear and faith, God and the Devil, and so forth.

"Reality is not something afar off. Reality is here and now, and when this is realized then will come peace---not as the world gives its peace, for that peace comes out of war and conflict, the peace that is eternal and everpresent, coming only from God. Then our relationship will be one of happiness through understanding."

He paused reflectively and then continued: "With the personal self there is always pain and conflict in relationship. But when man discerns his illusions man will find the unlimited, the 'Beloved,' within himself. Then his affection will be free from attachment, free from possessiveness and glorious in Its expression, for he will know his neighbour to be himself.

"Whatsoever you do unto the least of these so you do unto Me."

Then silence enveloped us both, and, in that silence, transformation was taking place within. I was no longer the same person as when I met him. All the things that were preventing true expression were being dissolved. It was this transformation that I was experiencing at that moment. My happiness was incomparable. I was no longer seeking or searching in anxiety. I was freed from a burden that had weighed me down since I was a boy.

That night I slept the sleep of freedom. Can you imagine a truly free sleep? It has to be experienced to be understood.

The following morning we were up before sunrise, knowing that we had still many miles to do. We were on our way as the sun was rising. I have always been thrilled by the sunrise and sunset, and that morning everything looked to me so beautiful and peaceful. The sky was blue and a calm blanket of clouds was covering the valley. It was cold, yet no wind, though any time now it might rise and perhaps become a hurricane.

Both of us were now dressed in the robe of the lama. Many lamas were coming and going and, as we passed, we blessed each other according to custom. We were now free from the gazing eyes of others for we were dressed in that distinguished familiar garb of the highly respected lama whom the people are taught to reverence.

My friend asked: "Do you think you could do a double distance to-day?"

"Yes," I answered, "I feel exceedingly strong now." (I was thin, having shed surplus flesh, and my muscles were like steel.)

"Yes," he said, "I can see that you have gained tremendous stamina."

"Well," I agreed, "you cannot be a weakling when travelling over these mountain passes, and I have become almost an expert."

We were travelling light, having left everything in Ok Valley. Just a few things we took in a haversack which we carried on our backs.

We passed along the lakeside where hundreds of yak and goats were having their morning meal. At the end of the lake we came to a river, and beyond it was a vast valley.

Dotted here and there were large black tents, the tents of the nomads, who are like the Bedouins, a fearless good-looking type of people. Around them were their flocks of yaks and sheep.

Chapter X

When we reached the floor of the valley these nomads came to welcome us, and my friend (who was a Geshi) blessed them. We partook of some food with them as is the custom.

Everywhere, when we came across a village or a company of nomads, we were made more than welcome, and if we stayed under their roof for a night that place was hallowed.

My friend said to me: "These people, the nomads, wander all over Tibet; they live in these yak hair tents, which as you see, are large and black. They are black because of the smoke that comes from their fires, which more often than not are made from yak dung and dry grass and are lit inside the tent."

"But might it not burn the tent down?"

"No, you see it is in the centre, and they sleep around it."

My friend said that we were on a long journey and we must be on our way, so the head nomad or chief brought out some clear liquid, which looked like water to me. Whe I drank it I thought I was on fire! It was spirit made from maize and barley. I felt the glow of my fingertips, and I said to my friend: "I think we should take some of that stuff along with us."

"No," he replied, "there will be plenty of it along the way, and it is not advisable to have too much when you are not accustomed to it."

I thought to myself that it was better than some whisky I knew of, and I could not help laughing at the memory of my father. When he was offered whisky, the usual thing is to take water with it, but when the water was brought to him he would say: "There is enough water in it already."

Chapter X

There is another story of a Scot who went to see the doctor. When the doctor had examined him he said: "My advice to you, Mr. McPherson, is to give up drinking whisky."

Mr. McPherson got up, and, as he was going out the door, the doctor called him back and said: "Mr. McPherson, you have forgotten something." "No, I don't think so," said McPherson.

"Oh, yes, you have forgotten my fee of three guineas for my advice." "Oh," exclaimed McPherson, "but 'am no' taking your advice."

These black tents were the only shelter the nomads had, summer and winter. The clothes they wore were woven by themselves from yak hair and wool, and some wore only a sheep-skin with the wool to the inside. All their garments were covered with thick grease.

When they get a new garment they grease it up with rancid yak butter and they use the same thing on their bodies; you can imagine what their clothes looked like, for at no time do they use water except for drinking.

Their meat is usually dried meat, dried in the sun similar to the biltong that is so popular in South Africa. Strips of the dried meat are hung up inside the tent.

The nomads grow peas, and corn and barley, and with their large herds of yak, sheep, goats, donkeys and a number of shaggy Tibetan ponies, it made a picture I would not have liked to miss.

The following day we reached the town of Gyantse, which is surrounded by mountains on all sides. Beyond the town we could see the monastery on the mountain slope surrounded by a great wall on all sides. At the top, at the right-hand side, was a huge wall where the holy carpet is hung for a few hours once a year. This carpet took eleven years to make, so I was told. It measures approximately one hundred feet by one hundred feet, with a huge picture of the Buddha in the centre.

My friend, being well known to the Geshi of Gyantse Monastery, told him of our sojourn, and we were made welcome; we stayed there for the night. This monastery is similar to all the monasteries with the exception that in the centre was a huge chorten or shrine (60 feet high) depicting the five elements, earth, water, air, fire and ether. The top portion of this chorten was plated with solid gold.

In the morning just as the sun rose the lamas were chanting *Om Mani Padme Hum* and we were given the blessing of the Buddha for a safe journey, for it was from here that we should soon be leaving civilisation behind. The track to the right led to Lhasa and the track to the left to Shigatse, These being the normal trade routes. The route we were going to take was over the Yung Pass, nearly 18,000 feet above sea level, and this area was mostly uninhabited.

So we set off with many blessings and were each given a prayer-flag called tungha. As we went down the valley we could still hear the lamas chanting and the boom of the great gongs and the sound of the *chonghas*. It would seem that we were being given a farewell by over 2,000 lamas.

We crossed the Yung Pass about midday, and a howling blizzard was blowing on the pass. In some parts the snow was several feet deep, and in the narrow path and other parts we were up to our waists in the deep snow, It was hard going and if I had not had previous experience it would have been impossible. I could see why so many had perished in these passes.

On the other side of the pass we reached a small village which is known by the name of Yakpeo. We were made welcome in one of the best of these peasants' houses.

Chapter X

The ground part of the house was used to shelter the animals, yaks, donkeys, poultry.

The loft above in which we slept had a stove in the middle. It was a unique experience.

Everybody, male and female, slept on the floor together. The donkeys neighed all night and you could hear the yaks chewing the cud. In the far corner of the loft was a square hole in the floor where these peasants sat to relieve themselves. The droppings fell into the muck below and were trampled in by the yaks and donkeys. How I wished then I had plugs for my nose and ears to keep out smell and noise; and it was not surprising that next morning I said to my friend that I would rather sleep in the open in future. No huts were provided for travellers in this out-of-the-way part of the country, as nobody used to pass in this direction.

I was glad to be on my way again, for I had not yet the power to make myself oblivious to these conditions. We crossed several rivers on the way, some of them rushing with great rapidity towards the great Tsang Po, with ice and snow mixed with the water. At parts there were shallows, and at these we crossed. By now I had become accustomed to the wet and cold; this was an everyday occurrence, and only the strongest could survive. But the anticipation of being with the great sage of Ling-Shi-La was sufficient to carry me on my way rejoicing.

The following day we reached the great Tsang Po, otherwise called the great Brahmaputra, the oldest and holiest river in the world. We were on the steep mountainside, and far below was the Tsang Po, the one river I wanted to see, as it contained the ice and snow coming from the great Himalayas through the ages past. This river was about a quarter of a mile wide, and the noise of the roaring water was terrific as it rushed through the gorges. It was dangerous going, for a false step would send us hurtling into the deep roaring water below.

Eventually we reached the bed of the river, the sides of which were covered with wild flowers, and on the slopes were wild roses, rhododendron bushes and wild poppies in rare profusion, hardly looked upon by human eyes.

I said to my friend: "This alone is worth coming to see."

We had not spoken for hours. We did not have the opportunity to do so, as we had to travel in Indian fashion most of the way, because of the dangerous going.

We camped on the side of the river for the night, as it was getting late, and it would be impossible to travel in the dark. Besides, Padong was still some miles away. There we would cross the Tsang Po---how, I did not know. Anyway I was content to leave it at that.

While searching around, my friend came upon a cave, and to our surprise a solitary man was there. My friend asked him: "How long have you been here?"

He replied: "Twenty-five years, to-day." It was co-incidence that we should arrive on that very day.

"What does he live on?" I inquired.

"Oh, fish and various roots he knows of." my friend replied. "There is good fishing in the Tsang Po."

This man recognised my friend as one of the living Masters and wanted to follow us.

Chapter X

He was a fine-looking man, one of the nomads who had by some means struck upon the science of the occult. My friend was struck by his bearing and his obvious sincerity. He told him that it was impossible for us to take him with us as we were on a special mission.

Then my friend asked: "What have you accomplished in your twenty-five years?"

He replied: "I can walk across the Tsang Po."

"Is that all?"

"Yes."

"Well," said my friend, "what a waste of time?"

Then he told the man something of what I myself had learned in the short time I had been with him. This made the devotee all the more keen; he seemed to have made up his mind that soon he would be ready to come to my friend, who nodded in assent of this desire and said: "When you are ready I will come for you. My sanctuary is at Zamsar, away beyond Lhasa by the Kya Chu River. One day you will find the pearl of great price, my son."

We left him there staring after us, for in his heart was the impelling desire to know the Truth. I looked back and gave him a wave; and we went on our way.

How everything was provided for us in the way of food and shelter amazed me, but my friend had absolute faith. I had often doubted, but he never. I used to say to myself: "I wish I had your faith, I could move mountains." At times he would get my thought and he would say: "You will." These two words rang in my ears, for at that moment I knew why he was the Master of every situation.

Chapter X

We rested about a mile farther down the river for the night. We had fish for supper, also for breakfast next day. How my friend managed to get the food I do not know to this day; I felt I could not ask him.

We were now only five miles from Padong, and we reached it in four hours after we had set out. The going was hard and dangerous, and one mile in just over three-quarters of an hour was slow work for us who could do about twenty miles in a day.

Few people had passed this way. In some places there was no track at all. I wondered how we were to cross the Tsang Po and said so to my friend, and he replied: "All has been provided!" Perhaps he was disappointed with me for my lack of faith. But my faith grew stronger, as one event after another proved that all was provided. There seemed to be an Intelligence behind all things, great and small, even the smallest detail was taken care of, and I gradually reached the state of mind in which I knew that this was so and eventually I had the assurance too. I knew there was an Intelligence that ruled the Universe and that the same Intelligence was ruling us also, and being perfect in Itself I knew that no detail would be missing. This has been with me ever since.

Therefore I do not plan but leave it to the Intelligence; everything works out a thousand times better than if I had planned it myself. When I did plan I found I had to continue replanning. I then realised that when I planned, things did not turn out anything like when the intelligence that knows the how of all things was leading me. It was a case of "Lead, Kindly Light, lead Thou me on. I do not want to see, one step enough for me, lead Thou me on." The words of the Master came so often to me, "What I see the Father do I do likewise," which means action with faith knowing that a perfect Intelligence is guiding every move even to the smallest detail.

Chapter X

When we reached Padong I could see no means by which we could cross the Tsang Po, for here it was well over a quarter of a mile wide. My friend said. "Sit down here!" He was silent for a few minutes, and then said: "We will have a coracle here in a few minutes."

No sooner had he said this than a Tibetan carrying a coracle over his head came out from nowhere.

(A coracle is a boat, or a kind of boat, made of bamboo covered with yak skin tightly sewn together and spread over the bamboo sticks which makes it into a sort of square boat three feet deep and about five feet wide, and seven feet in length. The amount that these contraptions carry is amazing. Another type of boat the use is the log of a tree with all the inside cut out; the bottom is then flattened, and the result is an excellent canoe.)

At this place the river is smooth, like a sheet of glass; there was only a slight ripple caused by the gentle breeze that was blowing. My friend went up to the man with the coracle and said: "Will you take us across the river to the other side?"

"Yes," answered the man, "the Hermit of Ling-Shi-La told me you would be here today, and I was just coming with the coracle when I saw you. My name is Pede Dong." My friend asked no further questions.

We got into the coracle and away we went, Pede Dong paddling for all he was worth, for though the water was smooth it was silently but swiftly flowing, the current being strong.

We reached the other side about half-a-mile down the river.

These coracles are light and are of various sizes; some are as much as 10 feet long by 8 feet wide and can be carried easily on the head and back; they weigh only about 85 lb. to 95 lb.

Chapter X

Now we were on virgin soil, a part of Tibet which had not yet been explored, yet there were numbers of yaks, goats and sheep. The nomads were there with their great mastiff dogs to protect the flocks from the snow leopards and the wolves which at night come down to devour what then can find. These fierce mastiff attack and skill these marauders.

These dogs would not hesitate to attack a stranger and destroy him. So we kept one eye open. Eventually we got on to a track which would take us over a high pass. Pede Dong told us it was 19,000 feet above sea level and that the winds were so strong that no living soul had ever crossed it, except the Hermit himself who lived beyond in the valley, a valley which was said to be the most beautiful in all Tibet.

My friend took the lead, as he always did, this time with a determined look; he knew what was in front of us.

He turned round to me and said: "You know that legends are told about places as these.

Some of them are true, some are just legends, but I think there is some truth in the legend about this pass."

"Look!" he exclaimed. And there on top of the pass we could see the snow whirling up into the sky as the hurricane wind tore into it. If I had been by myself I would never have tackled the journey but I knew that the faith of my friend would overcome all obstacles.

With steady steps and strong wills we trudged on, climbing, climbing, climbing. I wondered how much more. We had left the woodline now and were in the open, and as we entered the snows the wind blew fiercer and fiercer. I thought: "Will we ever reach the top of this pass alive?"

Chapter X

We had to pick our way, as there was no real path to guide us, just a goat track here and there; one goat track would lead one way and one another, but my friend always picked the right one.

The snow was extremely deep, but the surface was hard with the continual freezing, and it held fast. I wondered, should the crust break, how far I would sink into the snow beneath me. Like Peter on the water, I was wondering. My friend must have caught my thought, for he said: "The snow is like a rock under your feet!"

The wind by this time was terrific; it was forced up between the mountains on each side which formed a funnel through which it gained momentum. As one gust followed another it was just as if a gigantic force was pushing the wind through the gap that separated the towering snow-clad mountains on each side. The sight was certainly glorious but it was an awe-inspiring one. The great glaciers, those rivers of ice, could be seen forcing their way down the mountainside, crunching their way to the valley below.

For a while we took shelter in a short of cave by the way, and watched the aweinspiring scene, when we heard a thunderous noise. We looked up, and lo! a gigantic avalanche of snow and ice was tearing everything before it. Millions of tons of snow and ice thundered down the face of the mountain into the deep ravine where other avalanches had gone before.

"A sight for the gods alone," I said, "for no one could ever pass this way."

My friend did not answer; I did not think that he was worried---I knew him better than that. At last he said: "Let us go on."

We had reached two-thirds of the way to the top of the pass when he stopped. "Look!" he exclaimed, and there we could see the Hermit about two hundred feet below us on the rock face. We could hear him calling us not to go further up but to climb down on to the face of the rock and on the right side, and there we would find no wind blowing. We did so and reached a ledge that ran along the mountainside for about two hundred yards. Then we saw the valley below; a more gorgeous sight I have never seen. Anyway in the distance was a lake, in the middle of which there was an island, and on that island was a house, exactly as I had seen it in my reverie. The valley was pale green, covered with a carpet of wild flowers of varying colours; the lake also looked a pale green, reflecting the valley and the snowcapped mountains surrounding it. Lower down, the mountains were covered with wild roses and rhododendron bushes in full bloom.

"What a wonderful sight!" I said to my friend, "the Hermit has the loveliest place in all the world, and no one has seen it but himself."

Here and there I could see wild yaks and wild donkeys grazing peacefully in the valley, and I was eager to get farther down when we again heard the Hermit's voice this time calling: "Be careful and be patient, and watch for falling rocks above you. The goats sometimes dislodge a rock which sends an avalanche of rocks down the mountainside. You are protected and all will be well."

I knew then that all would be well. We got down easily now to where the Hermit was.

There was rejoicing at our meeting in the flesh.

I said: "How is it that there is no wind here?" and he replied: "Look at the formation of the rocks; do you see those great rocks jutting out above you?" I looked up and saw great jutting rocks.

"The wind," he explained, "is deflected above these and leaves this area free; that is why no living soul has crossed that pass, and this is the only way, my secret way, into my valley."

"What about the the other side?" I asked.

"That is even more difficult to enter," he replied.

"All the valley to yourself! How wonderful!"

"The time," he said, "will come when the valley will be populated; people will eventually find their way here. At present it is hallowed ground. Heaven and earth here are joined together. Only spiritual beings and those who can travel in the astral have access, and I may tell you there are many."

We wended our way down together, and the rest of the way was easy. We reached the edge of the lake, and the beauty was unsurpassable. The foilage was even more beautiful than I first thought. The over-all shade was a soft pale mossy green and by the side of the lake was a coracle. We got into it and the Hermit paddled us across his island sanctuary.

Never shall I forget the sight. Natural foilage filled the area, right up to the edge of the natural green grass lawns, which some sheep and goats kept short by eating lusciously. Then came palm trees which seemed to have been planted and specially cared for. I could see that they were of the same species that studded the natural foilage. The Hermit said that these grew from slips which he had planted and, as they grew, he tended them so as to make them into a regular formation. At the foot of the palms were wild flowers and large Chinese poppies of a very delicate blue, and in the centre of all this was built a charming house of stones neatly fitted together. The roof was constructed from bamboo covered with thatch made from palm leaves, and inside was a beautifully clean floor made from fine sandstone taken from the rock nearby.

The furniture was made of bamboo and grass worked into exquisite designs.

There was also cooking utensils which he had brought over from Gyantse on his many trips in and out of his sanctuary. The couches were made of bamboo with grass knitted tightly into various designs. As I sat on one I said: "This is comfort personified."

He built the fire of dry wood gathered from the island and with the use of a piece of flint and a piece of steel he lit dry leaves and blew them into a blaze. The he laid the wood upon it and in a few minutes there was a lovely, comforting fire.

I said: "You are a very self-contained person!"

"Yes," he explained, "but my work takes me all over the world, Just as you saw me in Ok Valley so I travel everywhere, healing and influencing minds towards peace and happiness.

You will learn much of that here with me, my son."

His long grey hair and beard and his deep set eyes shining brilliantly with intelligence gave him a dignity of bearing seldom possessed by any living person. His look contained the wisdom of the ages. He stood over six feet, and he gave one the feeling of a mental as well as a physical giant. I said to myself: "This is truly the wisest man in all Asia."

CHAPTER XI

As we sat round the fire for a little while talking, there was a sense of perfect harmony. We all felt as if we were one family. There was nothing strange or strained as there usually is at a first meeting and I felt that much more would be revealed to me here.

Although we had done the journey in six days, which is just half the time it would ordinarily have taken, I did not feel tired. There was such an atmosphere of peace all around us.

I felt exhilarated---yet I could do with a wash! The Hermit must have sensed my feeling, for he said: "Take that path there," pointing to a path that led down to the lake, "and you will find a pool in which you can bathe; the water is warm. There is a hot spring at the edge of the island and the hot water runs into the pool which I have made, only be careful not to go too near the spring itself because it is boiling, and while you are having a bathe and wash-up I will get supper ready."

My friend and I then walked down the path. At the sides all the way down were wild flowers, especially Chinese poppies of exquisite colours and very large, the largest I had ever seen. When we reached the lake we could see at the side a bubbling spring of boiling water which ran into the lake. Here the Hermit had built two walls out into the lake which kept the hot water in an area of about thirty feet or more before it merged into the lake of cold water.

I stripped, got in and swam to the end of the channel between the two walls. The water near the spring was hot but as I got farther out it became cooler until it reached cold water. The water here was clear and I could see many fish swimming round.

I said to my friend: "What an ingenious contraption, hot and cold water at call. The Hermit has everything to his hand. What a wonderful place! Put this down in the middle of England or America and thousands of people would be swarming to it every year."

We swam about in the pool---I do not know for how long---when we heard the Hermit calling: "Supper is ready!"

I said: "What do you think he has got for supper?"

"That will be a surprise," came the reply---and indeed it was. There, laid on the table, were grilled fish, fresh butter and plenty of milk, and bread which he had made himself.

"Where in all the earth did you get this bread?" I exclaimed.

"Oh," he smiled, "you will see my corn and barley fields to-morrow and my little mill with which I crush the corn and barley."

The fish was delicious, and the bread was made from mixed barley and cornmeal and it had a nutty texture. I never tasted such excellent bread before, and the butter was as fresh as if it had just come from the churn.

I turned to my friend and asked: "Did you ever taste anything like this?" It was a good meal and we enjoyed it, for we had not eaten since early that morning.

Supper over, we sat by the fire again and talked about the things we had done. This pleased the Hermit, and he said: "You are the first two people that have ever entered my sanctuary, and you, my son," looking at me, "you are the first person from the outer world who has had the privilege of being taught by the great Masters on all the Sciences of the occult."

"Yes," I said, "it is a great privilege and I am indeed grateful to you for your very kind invitation and welcome to this wonderful sanctuary of yours."

"Nothing happens by chance, my son," he said. "Many have been called but few are chosen. You have followed that for which you were born; few ever do, the world has swallowed them up."

I thought to myself: "What an apt term, for it nearly swallowed me up too."

"You have come here because it was ordained that you should," he continued. "Your work is unique and the world needs your message, but you have to be prepared for greater things to come. You will also write books, of a kind that has never been written before. Books have been written by others, but they do not help man to know himself."

"We have been watching over you for a long time," he added, "both those who are in the flesh and those who are out of the flesh."

I said: "I do not feel worthy of all this."

"We are not concerned with your worthiness; we are concerned only with how the Truth can best be made known to the world. You are a good instrument and we know that you will be a better one after this."

Then he said: "As your time is limited, I do not intend that you should waste any of it, so we will start working right away. To-night I would like to instruct you on certain matters pertaining to the work before the actual practice.

"What is necessary to a consciousness that is clear is not only a free mind, freed from all that is false, but also a consciousness that is creative. The mind is the instrument but it is the consciousness that has creativeness. Your consciousness," he said, "is like point which has the totality of all Creativeness behind it, and your thought expressed is in exact proportion to your state of consciousness. If your consciousness is caught up in mental images, beliefs, and suchlike, then your creativeness is smothered up because the consciousness is caught up in your beliefs, your ideas. your images, your authorities and formulations, and you will note that these are not creative.

"Now you must learn here through practice that your consciousness can move in space and is creative at any point in space you desire, because the totality of all Creativeness is behind it.

"You do not know what your consciousness is, therefore you do not know what Creativeness is, but your consciousness cannot be separated from the totality of all Creativeness in the Universe, for there is only one Consciousness, there cannot be two, neither can there be two Creators. Your consciousness then is the point through which Creativeness works and is the point through which you express Creativeness.

"Now, if your consciousness is caught up in a mind that is confused with ideas, it will merely express this condition, and you will not know what is true and what is false. What is in the mind is not creative. Creativeness is beyond the mind, in a consciousness that is free from the confusion of ideas."

I said: "I am beginning to see further 'now'."

My friend was also attentive, and I could see that he also was amazed at the wisdom of the Hermit.

"Therefore your consciousness," he went on, "is like a broadcasting station through which the Creator is sending His perfect vibrations outwardly in all directions. These vibrations move through your mind, brain and nervous system, affecting the heart, glands, lungs, vasomotor system and all organs of the body, thus registering its effects there, and then go out beyond the confines of the individual into the world of ether that few know and understand.

"It is only the idea of age that makes you old, because you are expressing the idea of age and not the Creativeness that is Eternal and Ever-present." This was a response to my thought, for I was thinking at the moment, "I wonder how old you are."

Then he said: "The Creative vibrations rush out into the atmosphere on their creative mission, harmonising everything.

If your consciousness is caught up in your ideas, your fixed beliefs, then it is your ideas and beliefs that are being expressed and not the Creativeness that alone is creative. Your ideas are not creative because you do not know whether they are true or not." When he said this I looked at my friend for it was he who had first said these words to me.

Now I could see that I was being taken further along the way to Truth. I could feel the transformation but could not explain it. Yet I knew it to be true and it was not an idea, because I could not make an idea of it. What I created in my mind did not matter, because what was in my mind could not be the Truth. Truth was beyond mind but I knew It to be my Real Self. I was aware only in my consciousness and, when free, I was creative.

Then he said: "Man is not a mere physical being, he is in Reality, a centre of consciousness in the totality of all Consciousness. Now this must not be a mere idea, and you must not try to form an idea of it, because then you will lose It, nor must you try to form an idea in your mind of what I say. What I am trying to do is to clear the consciousness, so that That which *Is* Real can manifest."

I realised that what he was pointing to was beyond mind. Divine reason would lead me to that which was beyond reason, beyond mind.

"If your thought waves merely carry the vibration of your conditioning, then you have done nothing. But when your consciousness is freed, then the Creativeness that created all things will express Itself without effort, because being effortless there is no resistance, no confusion, no conditioning, no reaction, only pure action.

"There is no such thing as ignorance or fear in the Creativeness. Ignorance and fear exist only in man's mind through lack of understanding, and therefore have no existence outside man's mind. But when the Creativeness becomes active and free through a clear consciousness it sweeps through the billions of cells in the body, creating Its own natural rhythm. Thus the Creator and His Creation becomes One."

I said: "I have heard those last few words before, but now they seem different."

"There you go again," he said, "you are merely super-imposing another idea on the one you had before, only because this one looks better than the last one. Is that not so? This is not an intellectual discussion; it is a transforming process."

I thought to myself: "How can I get over this?"

He said: "Let it all drop from your mind; free your consciousness from the intellect---the intellect does not know what is true and what is not true. Life's Creativeness is *Now,* the intellect only speculates about It. Creativeness is now! If it is not *now,* It will never be, because you do not create It."

"I do not want you to make an idea of what I say to you," he went on, "I do not want you to make what I say to you a mere belief, for then it will be just another belief a little better than the previous one."

Chapter XI

I was now beginning to understand myself, my ideas, my beliefs, my images. I could now see that none of this could ever be the truth, nor could I make it the truth. Truth was the Living Creativeness beyond the mind and would express Itself more as I understood that which was hindering Its true expression.

"When you accept me as an authority," he went on, "or any other authority, then you will begin to fear, and confusion will result. Then you will express that confusion both in your mind and body and beyond, and that is not Truth.

"Love is something you cannot define. Love is Creativeness in action. Love is Creative action. Ideas and beliefs can only create reaction, and reaction can never be Creative action.

Creative action is the expression of Divine Consciousness within the individual consciousness that realises It through freedom, the Individual consciousness being the point through which the Divine Consciousness expresses Itself. Thus the individuality is dissolved into pure action, for there is only 'One.' Now you see it is the self that hinders the pure action of Love.

"The release of this Divine Energy through your consciosness will harmonise your mind and body and also those whom you hold in your consciousness at that moment of realisation. The Creator and His Creation become 'One.'

"This delightful effect sweeps through the cells, establishing the Divine Rhythm. There is relaxation, comfort, peace and joy. Possessiveness and fear pass away, for such arise only from human desires."

He paused for a moment and then went on: "The one who is freed will soon become aware of the effect of a wave of anger or aggressiveness because that one feels the inharmony, not that it affects him in any way, but he becomes aware of it, and knows how false it is, having no power except that of the immature mind that is expressing it. It is only the small mind that engages in these false movements.

"Since various human thought-waves, such as of hate, jealousy, and fear have their effect upon the body, we see them also expressed in the facial muscles revealing the tortured mind that is hidden behind them."

"Now," he said, "here is the secret behind the change of form. Consciousness being creative, alone creates form and is capable of transformation of matter-form through the direction of the consciousness that is creative.

"Consciousness to be creative must be free, so that the 'Father can do the work.'

Whatever the Consciousness asks through a directing and understanding faith, the Father fulfills that direction, because there is no separation or hinderance.

"Therefore as the Divine Creativeness transforms the Eternal ever-existing Energy of the Universe into form, so does the individual consciousness that is aware of its unity with the totality of all Creativeness." What I see the Father do, I do likewise,'" I ventured to quote.

"Yes," he affirmed, "no matter in what form, mineral, vegetable, animal, human or angelic, Consciousness is Supreme.

"This is the secret teaching which Jesus gave to his disciples. Therefore all power is in the Divine Consciousness in heaven and on earth.

"Remember the Divine Idea is not a human idea; a human idea is a mental image, but the Divine Idea is the manifestation of the Divine Itself. 'I and the Father are one.' These words you yourself know, but to many they are mere words because their consciousness is a prisoner in their own creations, and they only bring the idea into their self-created prison, the doors and bars being their ignorance.

"The Divine Idea is the 'word' of Creation and must ever remain the same perfect Creative Word, the form changing into greater splendour to reveal the Divine Idea. Therefore the vibration of Love is the keynote of perfect Creation and the rhythmic organisation of atoms into more perfect form.

"Therefore you see that a clear consciousness is not bound up in human ideas but is the point through which the Divine Creativeness acts to combine the ether atoms, to form the pattern of the Divine Ideas.

"There is an Intelligent Force, a knowing-how, that induces magnetic attraction which binds the ether atoms as the basis of the form to be manifested in the realm of the physical atoms which produce condensation, and the materialisation of the atoms to be seen by the physical eye."

"Now," he said, "to-morrow we will have definite practice in astral projection and according to the freedom of your consciousness, so will you move in the astral and each evening we can have further discussions."

And he added, "The sun has already set and you should retire for the night. To-morrow morning we will watch the sun rise and in the evening we will watch it set. I want you to see the whirling of the snow on the pass as the sun's rays strike it. It is truly a wonderful sight."

Chapter XI

"I can believe that from what I saw to-day," I said, "I love to see the sun rising and setting."

Around the main room there were small alcoves in which comfortable stretchers were fitted. So I retired for the night, knowing I should have a peaceful, satisfying sleep.

Next morning I was awakened by my friend tugging at me. I had not moved from the position in which I had lain the night before. He said: "Breakfast is ready."

I was soon up, shaved, dressed and fed, and we went out to see the sun rise. We watched it climb up from behind the pass. The snow was still whirling into the air and I could see the red glow behind it. It was like a gigantic white veil with all the colours of the rainbow showing through it, It was a sight I shall never forget as long as I live---the sheer wildness of it thrilled me through and through. The pass then became visible and I could see how impossible it would be to cross it. The comparison between the calm surface of the lake and the hurricane that was blowing nearly 19,000 feet high was like a clam sea, and a hurricane that would toss a giant liner as if it were a mere cork.

"Now," said the Hermit, "I want you to begin to learn the art of astral travel," and we went inside.

He directed me to lie down and relax every muscle and fibre in my body. I very soon found myself going into a semi-trance state. It was not a sleep because I was in a state of semiconsciousness.

I heard his voice say, "Let go of your body," and as I did so I could feel myself soaring above my body. I looked down at it where it lay and could see that I was free from it.

"Now," he said, "you must not fear anything or you will come back to your body instantly."

Chapter XI

I felt a calmness, the stillness of another world. I could still hear his voice saying, "You are in the astral now. Now think of the place you want to go to and the person or people you want to see and you will be there instantly."

I did so and to my wonderment I was there watching what was going on. I was now caught up in the activities of the people I was watching, and it was a queer sensation. In fact, I felt I was actually with them, though not in the physical.

I must have been so watching for about a quarter-of-an-hour, when I heard his voice again: "Now leave of your own will and come back." I did so and came back into my body with a memory of what I had seen.

"Now," he said when I got up, "you see your memory is not merely a part of your brain, but it interpenetrates your brain, in an astral counterpart. In fact there is even a finer interpenetrating body in which there is also memory, and this you will reach very soon."

Then he said: "I am convinced now that you have the ability to travel in the astral naturally, and soon you will travel further in the ether."

This practice went on for days, and each night we discussed the work I had to do. Then one day he said: "We will now travel together, this time out into the ether of space."

This, however, was not so successful at first, but after some practice I could master it and said: "Interplanetary travel is already accomplished in the ether; some day it will be done in the physical."

I knew now how the Hermit could come to a seance while living in the physical body.

Chapter XI

To him there was no space. Later I made inquiries about those whom I visited and what they were doing, and every detail I had stated of them was correct. They were amazed at my knowing so much about their movements.

I was warned, however, by the Hermit never to travel in the astral for curiosity, but only to help those in need. In many instances since then, people have seen me at their bedside when they wanted help, and this was to me further proof of my ability to travel in the astral.

A certain Doctor W---, a friend of mine in Johannesburg, was startled to see me plainly in his room one night. When he told me of this I explained to him: "I was thinking deeply about you at that time." This was automatic travel and it is very helpful in healing work, and yet some people were upset at seeing me. Immediately I saw this I made myself invisible by the natural desire to do so, though I did not leave their proximity.

Since then I have been able to travel at will even while in the conscious state, and on nearly all occasions the healing power was felt by those who were being healed.

The Hermit was delighted with my progress and he explained it to me in this way: "What happens in healing work is, the inner mind is impressed, and the impression creates a subconscious activity through the nervous system affecting the generating cells and glands, and then all the cells of the body become active. Miraculous cures are effected in this way.

"These impulses travel in ever-widening circles, eventually affecting the whole of mankind. It churns into motion all the atoms and cells of the body, with the consequent transformation of the cells, and the reaction will be in exact proportion to the state of consciousness, because there is not separation.

"With the change in the rate of vibration in the body, the body reflects this activity upon the mind, and this produces a feeling of well-being.

"The very opposite takes place with man himself when in fear. This unnatural vibration upsets the natural equilibrium and when a man is ignorant of the cause more fear enters and adds fuel to the fire which man has already kindled by his negative thought-action."

He paused and then: "You see," he said, "when man is caught up in his own conditioning and is influenced by his surroundings , his mind reacts to these conditions---when he fails to understand himself and the cause of his conditioning.

"Man's consciousness permeates the whole of his mind and body. When he fails to understand that he has his roots in Reality which is Superconscient, where the totality of all unconditioned Intelligent Energy exists, he flounders in his fear because he is ignorant of his true nature."

"Then," I said, "man's consciousness, when free, really exists beyond the confines of his body."

"Yes," he replied, "you see consciousness is firstly expressed through the mind, and then comes the influencing of the body through the brain and nervous system. The first nerve plexus rules the heart, lungs and glands, and other parts of the body. The cranial nerves are responsible for the transmission of the vibration of light, sound, and feeling that come from the external world and these must be interpreted without fear through understanding.

"The consciousness also moves downwards into the emotional life of the individual through the solar plexus and then into the lower vitals to the physical, then to the total activity of the animal, vegetable and mineral kingdoms---the Subconscient. Here all action that is behind all mineral, vegetable and animal planes is controlled and directed. Man's consciousness encounters all the highest in the Superconscient to the lowest in the Subconscient."

"Yes," I remarked, "I can see that the whole is under the direction of the

Consciousness---Life being Consciousness and Intelligence acts through the mind-substance.

Divine Consciousness, Intelligence and Substance are One."

"Yes," he agreed, "but man, being ignorant of the Subconscient activity as a beneficent natural instinctive force, sees evil and as the result creates his own hell and the devil is himself."

"You see," he went on, "the lower vital belongs to the part of the nervous system from the solar plexus downward. This includes the animal, vegetable and mineral kingdoms which are subsconscious in man. The Subconscient activity belongs to the totality of all action in the mineral, vegetable and animal kingdoms and is subconscious in man."

He continued: "When the consciousness becomes aware, it frees itself from the fear which is engendered through being ignorant of the activity of these forces. Man has been given dominion over all things above and below, but few have gained this understanding."

"Now," I exclaimed, "I see that the whole activity is 'One' but man has divided it up in his own mind, and then what he fears, he produces just as he fears."

"Yes," he said, "through the whole of the animal nature there is one complete mental activity which belongs entirely to this plane. The same with the vegetable and the mineral.

Man's consciousness is the ruling factor in them all. All wild animals are controlled by man's consciousness when he knows himself, his thoughts, and his reactions, and when he understands his feelings and desires, his beliefs, his ideas, and how they are formulated in his mind. When ignorant of this he falls into the error of seeing a power that is evil or a power that is greater than himself and he begins to fear nature. He sees a power that is good and one that is evil, and so he eats of the fruit of the Tree of Knowledge of Good and Evil and dies in his sin, his sin being his ignorance."

"Yes, I see now," I said, "I see that our emotions, fears, hates, anger and jealousy, and such-like, all arise from our ignorance of the Subconscient, and when not understood affect the whole body function. Through our senses we acquire conflicting ideas which we cannot correlate. Thus we have a confused mind."

"Yes," he said, "your fears, your beliefs, your mental conflicts affect the whole organism. Thus the whole of the Subconscient within the individual becomes confused, with the result that the body suffers; then the body talks back to the mind. The mind, unaware of what the cause is, succumbs to the unnatural state of the body. Paul says it is Eve that is deceived."

"Oh, I see," I replied, "Eve represents the soul and Adam the body. So Eve is deceived and Adam, being the body must suffer as a consequence."

"Yes," he said, "you have it; truly you have it."

He added: "You see, my son, as you have already learnt through your training, the Spirit-Consciousness in man is free, and although incarnate in the flesh It is still free, otherwise It could never be free. Freedom is your natural state; it is your conditioning that is unnatural, created by yourself.

221

Chapter XI

"The easiest and quickest way man can find this freedom is through love and understanding. The Subconscient is not evil in itself, it is the means of man's growth. But man attaches evil ideas to it, with the result that he begins to fear what he does not know. But what does he fear? He fears his own ideas and is caught up in his own conditioning. Only when he begins to realise that it is his own ideas that he really fears does he free himself from his own creations and becomes consciously free, and then he thinks purely. Then the Spirit- Consciousness which is Divine can transform his mind and body by Its own Eternal Presence."

"Man is the image and Likeness of his Creator, he cannot be otherwise, because God is all there is and we cannot exist apart from Him.

"So, you see, my son, It is the Unknown alone that is creative. What is known can never be creative, for the creative ever remains unknown. What you know is relative-external created, and can never be creative.

"Others who know nothing of the Truth merely give you an idea, but that, you see, is relative and you merely imitate their ignorance. When you realise this and discern the falseness of it, then the Creative, the Unknown, will be revealed, but will still remain unknown. Thus you will find the Unknown within you, but never external to yourself, my son. I cannot tell you what It is; no one can. Others can give you only an idea of It and this is not the Creative.

The Creative is your own Livingness."

I sat back and again thought to myself: "Truly, he is the wisest man in all Asia."

CHAPTER XII

It was a month since I arrived at the Hermitage of Ling-Shi-La and I had gained more than I had ever hoped for. The days were an ever-increasing joy to me, and a deep affinity had grown up among the three of us.

My friend who had met me at Kalimpong was now my constant companion and I decided to stay with him for the rest of the time left to me. His Sanctuary was beyond Lhasa, at a place called Zamsar, and we had many talks about it. We talked also about what the Hermit had said and my friend gave me much enlightenment on points I could not then grasp.

My friend's sanctuary was 200 miles away from the Hermitage of Ling-Shi-La. The journey there together, and the experience and joy of the companionship, will have to be told in another book which I hope to write later.

I had grown to love the Hermit during my stay with him and he felt the affection I had for him, for it was returned a hundredfold. I was his son, his true Spiritual son, and we both felt the same way. To me he was a true Spiritual father, and when I told him so his eyes would light up with joy, and I could feel the flow of that love that is beyond human understanding coming from him as he put his arm around my shoulders.

He was the sage of sages and I drank in every word he said. My friend also felt that warmth of love coming from the Hermit, although an adept himself he respected the wisdom of the sage of sages and listened with an attention not known to the ordinary man.

The joy of this true Spiritual companionship cannot be expressed in words, for there are no words coined to reveal the true meaning.

Chapter XII

In a few days I would be leaving with my friend on our long journey over the roof of the world. He himself had come all the way to Kalimpong to meet me, nearly three hundred miles. His adeptship was second to none; he had a deep understanding of all that was false, and it was this that at the beginning helped me most. To cast off the burden that I had carried so long put my feet on the first rung of the ladder on which I have climbed steadily ever since.

During the last few days we fished on the lake for food only, the Hermit's desire being that we should take only for our needs from day to day.

I asked my friend: "How old do you think the Hermit is?"

"No one knows his age," he replied, "and he will not discuss it with anyone. But it is a very, very long time since he taught at Ganden monastery."

The Hermit was also an authority on rare plants and roots. He had a wonderful knowledge of the rarest plants and roots in all Asia, and he would explain to us what they were and their uses.

The rarest of these plants, he said, grew only in the highest mountain regions, and the difficulty of locating them, together with the hardships experienced in the mountain regions, prevented all except the most experienced climbers possessed of maximum endurance to reach the coveted prize.

I said that I would like to search for these plants. I had always been keen on searching for the unobtainable, and I was eager to go searching. My friend looked at me as much as to say, "Do you know what you are letting yourself in for?"

Anyway, it was decided that we would try to find four of the rarest plants, and we set out with that purpose the next morning, each taking with us some food in a haversack and some warm headgear and gloves as a protection from the icy blasts of the high mountains. We also took climbing staffs, an ice axe and a rope in case we should need it, and a light spade with which to dig, in the snow.

The Hermit thought that the most likely place to find the plants would be up towards the pass, and we steadily made our way in that direction. I was amazed at the Hermit; he could outstrip us both and we were both experienced climbers. I had already climbed many passes, and even before coming to Tibet I had done much climbing in the New Zealand Alps, also in Europe.

It was getting dark when we reached the high levels above the woodline in the eternal snows. The Hermit said: "This is the time to find the Arhota; its root is the shape of a human body. It has a head, body, arms and legs, hands and feet, all represented by its roots. It has a flower that sparkles like a diamond; it can be found easier at night because it shines like a light in the snow. It grows underneath the snow many feet deep, yet it has the power to melt the snow around it and make its way to the surface. Its petals are white, like the snow, and if it did not shine and sparkle it would be impossible to locate it. It gives off a sort of phosphorescent glow."

"This plant," he added, "is used by the lamas as a general tonic for all ailments; the different parts of the root can be pulverised separately and used for the different parts of the body it represents."

We kept our eyes open, you may be sure, and we scanned the snow upon which the moon was now shining. The Hermit observed the Arhota first, and we dug down in the snow until we reached the root---and there, just as he had explained it, there it was with the shape of the human body.

It was exceedingly cold now and the winds were becoming very fierce.

Chapter XII

The Hermit said: "I think we had better practise Tumo for a while to generate heat in our bodies."

In an aside I asked my friend: "And does the Hermit practise Tumo, too?"

"Yes," he replied, "he is master of all the occult Sciences."

In a few minutes our bodies were like fire.

"In the morning we will look for the Ngodevwa, which is the flower of the angels," said the Hermit. "Its name is appropriate and, if we can find one, you will remember its beauty forever. This flower is also most difficult to obtain, as it grows deep underneath the snow. The only indication of its presence is a hole in the snow about six inches wide. It grows mostly where there is rock underneath. It generates a heat within itself and melts the snow all the way to the surface while it itself is hidden. We must find it before the sun rises, otherwise the hole gets hidden by the heat of the sun as the snow melts around it."

Again it was the Hermit who found the plant, the Ngodevwa. We dug down till we reached it, and I never saw anything so beautiful. It had a velvet surface, and the shine was impossible to describe completely. The petals were yellow, coming out of a deep purple centre with streaks of pink leading out into the centre of the petal right to the end. The petals were all of uniform size, with ends that came to a point dotted as if you had just painted them with pink and purple spots.

The Hermit prized this plant as one of the rarest in all Asia, and indeed it was a beautiful specimen. The root of this plant, he said, had never yet failed to cure kidney, bladder or dropsical conditions. When the lamas found this flower they used it very sparingly, even the smallest portion of it being effective.

Chapter XII

I was now getting more and more excited. We had been out a whole day and a whole night. We already had two meals and we had enough left for a third.

"Now," said the Hermit, "We will climb down to the rocks and there we hope to find the Chomdenda, which means "The conqueror." This plant grows out of the rock in the high rocky regions. Its roots has tremendous power, and we shall have to chop it virtually out of the rock. Its colour is grey and black, with a grassy stem, and at the end grows a grassy top."

"The properties of this plant," he went on to say, "are that it sustains you for days, even months. The lamas use it when crossing the mountains on long journeys. It has tremendous sustaining powers. The lamas believe that it has the power of the mountain rock in it, and some call it the "Elixir of Life.' It is brewed into a concoction with spirit made from corn, and it has the power to rejuvenate the cell structure, and it prevents wastage when the adepts are on a long practice of asceticism. The effects of a concoction of this plant, taken liberally, cause a deep trance or coma; the heart virtually ceases to beat, and suspended animation sets in. In this condition the body can be put into cold storage or buried deep in the snow for weeks. The Tibetan Yogi uses this concoction sometimes when he leaves his body in a cave and he wanders several weeks in the astral, and, when he comes back to his body, there is no wastage of any kind."

It was the Hermit again who found this plant, the Chomdenda, and he had to cut it from the rock with an ice axe.

"If you don't mind," I said to the Hermit, "I would like to take a bit of this with me."

We all laughed heartily, I didn't know for what, but we kept on laughing for some time. It was my friend who started us off. I asked him what we were laughing at and he replied: "You should know," But to this day I don't know!

"The last of the four rarest plants is called Yartsa Gumba," said the Hermit "it means summer grass and winter insect. The most extraordinary thing about it is that in winter it becomes a root and in the summer it becomes a caterpillar, and when the caterpillar becomes a root in the winter a flower grows out of its head. These plants are very scarce and are seldom found, but I think we may find one. We will look for it on the lower levels as we go down."

Sure enough the Hermit found it. "Now," he said, "this is just in-between summer and winter, and you see half of the caterpillar has already gone hard into a root, and you see the flower is beginning to come out of the head."

It was amazing to see the change taking place.

The properties of this animal plant have the effect of clearing the brain. When the lamas find this plant they use it to stimulate the brain centres so that they can stay awake for days without feeling the need for sleep. When on long journeys, in the winter snows, to sleep would be dangerous; anybody could be buried in the snow in no time. Also it is a strong nerve stimulant, and by using it the lama can travel for days without sleep or rest.

These rare plants fascinated me. Few people had any knowledge of them; certainly no one in the Western world had ever seen them. They may have heard of them, but I do now know of anybody having seen them.

We reached the Hermitage that evening---we had been away just two days and one night. The Hermit said it was a great achievement, for it took days, sometimes weeks, to locate the Arhota and the Ngodevwa.

Chapter XII

We had been travelling all the time except for eating and digging and I felt tired. I dived into the warm pool and swam around and felt quite fresh when I got back. We had supper and then retired for the night. I did not know it was morning until I felt the usual tugging of my friend.

Time was passing rapidly and I was feeling sad, for the parting was at hand. I felt I could stay here very much longer, but the Hermit said: "My son, you will have to go back soon into your world to do the work for which you were born."

"You are going to stay with your friend," he went on, "during the time that is left. Make the most of it. He will give you details whereas I have shown you the whole. This will be my last talk with you, my son." So we all sat down, eager to hear what he had to say, and this is what he said: "Divine reasoning and knowing the self will lead you out of the false. But even Divine reasoning must cease before you can experience that which is Real, for the Real is beyond reason, beyond the mind. To discern that which is false will enable you to free yourself from it.

"But, as I have already told you, the known is not creative, only the Unknown is creative. The known can never be the Unknown.

"You see, my son, in every nation, in every group, there is a conception of Reality which they call God. But this is just an intellectual approach to Reality-God. Most people are discussing Reality so as to discover what Reality is. Hence we have so many different philosophies, so many different groups and religions.

"Reality is the unknown and alone is creative---you understand that, my son?"

"Yes, I do," I humbly replied.

Chapter XII

"The mind cannot comprehend Reality, but you can translate Reality into your daily living by understanding that the only way to approach Reality is by true affection and love.

Then you will find yourself giving expression to Reality Itself; in this way you will translate Reality into your everyday living.

"Most people do not approach Reality through Love and affection but through antagonism and fear. Is it not so, that the members of a group while trying to approach Reality are antagonistic to the members of other groups? This is stupid nonsense, my son."

I was beginning to see more now; though the known was not Reality I still wanted a way to express It. I could now see that the key was in loving your neighbour as yourself.

"Is it not so, my son, that you have in the past tried to corner a bit of Reality for yourself?" he asked. "But it did not work. You desired Reality, only so that you could get what you wanted. Reality to you was but a means to an end. This is not expressing Reality; it is merely a suggestion in opposition to another suggestion in your mind.

"Now you know that the only way to express Reality is through love and affection, and then there is no frustration, no opposition. But this affection does not mean that you are merely in love with the idea that by so doing you will get what you want.

"People everywhere are seeking the love of God but hate their enemies. They are praying for peace but are preparing for war. They want success at the expense of their neighbour, but they are really cheating themselves.

"You see, my son, it is this inward poverty that makes them look to the external and they miss the Creativeness that is ever-present and Eternal.

"In the past you were discussing Reality as an idea, and so the idea became to you the Truth, when it was not the Truth."

I knew that now, for my friend very soon disposed of that fallacy with the first few words he said to me: "It does not matter very much whether it was true or not."

What I had was not the Real---and I knew it at that very moment, and I said so.

"True, my son." he affirmed.

Then he went on: "Nearly all literature on Truth or philosophies discusses Reality as an idea. Reality is Life, and the mind cannot conceive what It is, therefore it is useless trying to make an idea of Life. But when you see that an idea is but an imitation, a mental concept, it dies away. Then Life that is ever-present becomes a Reality in you. You do not create It; what you create is not Reality. Reality is not an idea or a mental formulation but an actual Livingness expressing Itself in Love and affection. As long as you have merely an idea of It you will never know or experience It.

"You must realise, my son, that you live because Reality lives. Reality is Life---the Unknown is Life, and Life is creative; you do not know what Life is but you know that It is."

"Yes," I said, "I do now know that It is, I am the Life."

"Yes," he interrupted, "provided you do not try to make an idea of It. You see, my son, if your prayers arise merely from an idea or a belief which is your own conditioning they amount to nothing. This conditioning must cease to be, before the Unknown comes into Being.

"You must never lose yourself in philosophy or question another on that which can be realised only by yourself. You see, my son, if I would philosophise to you about the wonders of Reality you would only build up an idea of Reality. But you can never give expression to Reality through an idea, only through the action of Love and affection.

"You do not know what Love is, but you can experience Love. Possessiveness is not Love. Love is Eternal and Ever-present, whereas possessive love comes to an end.

"God is the Unknown and cannot be known. The moment you think you know God it is not God you know, but an idea of God---a projected image which hinders the discovery of the Unknown."

"Yes, I can see that," I said, "at first I was afraid to throw away the false. My mind always wanted something to hang on to. But when I saw how false it all was and how my ignorance blinded me to the falseness of it, the false fell away. The freedom I felt was beyond words. I was no longer caught up in beliefs, in ideas; and my fears dissolved as I saw they were my own creations."

"Yes," he said, "that is all very true. *But Reality is never the result of the false, or the elimination of the false. You must know that It is now at this very moment and does not rise out of the false. The false has no foundation whatsoever; it is a myth. It is self-created illusion.*

"You see, my son, beliefs are a process of the mind and are born of the known. If you merely say 'God is the Unknown' you create an idea of the Unknown. But your mental creation of the Unknown is not the Unknown----the Creative---the Real.

Chapter XII

"The man who accumulates wealth, builds temples, organises religions; the bishops, the cardinals, the preachers, as well as the man who drops the bombs, say that God is their companion. Surely their belief is but a form of self-expansion. It is merely their own conceit.

Those who have conditioned their minds to a particular pattern which they call their religion can never realise the ultimate Reality which is Love and Affection."

"Yes," I said, "I can see that, and that is the cause of all antagonisms, each having a different pattern, a different religion, a different idea, trying to make others conform to their idea, and if they do not succeed they look upon you as something apart from themselves. The live in separation, which is the cause of all war, destruction and misery. They divided themselves into groups, nationalities, which is but a formulation in their minds. There is only one God, one Creator, and all must be His creation. The Creator and His creation are one."

"Yes," he said, "for the Unknown to Be, the mind must be completely emptied of what you believe or disbelieve. You must understand the whole content of your mind, the whole process of ideas and formulations, and by this means only will you be aware moment-to-moment, without any sense of accumulation. Your mind must be utterly silent without acceptance, without resistance, condemning or blaming; when the self has died then only is there that which is Real.

"Words are not important to you any more, for there is a state of Creativeness which is not an idea or a word or the expression of the self. You will then know what *Is*, what is Indescribable.

"A description of the Indescribable is merely a cultivation of memory. To verbalise the Indescribable---the Creative---the

Unknown, is to put It into time, and that, which is of time cannot be the Timeless."

"Now you see, my son," he said, "this knowing is not the result of the known but knowing that the known is not the Unknown---the Creative.

"It is not obtained through reason because It is beyond reason, but It does not run contrary to reason. It is not obtained through space or time factors, because It is ever-present in Its own Eternity. Therefore, every moment, all Life is concentrated at any point in Its omnipotence that you may choose to realise."

"Yes," I said, "I realise now that Divine Reason helps towards Divine Realisation. I can reason towards the Ultimate but reason must cease because it cannot go beyond mind.

When it knows that it can never know, at that moment there is Reality."

"Yes, my son, I see that you understand now, and *with this understanding you can go further, for there is no ending. Anything that has an end is not Reality.*

"It is the Unmanifest that gives rise to the manifest; the Invisible gives rise to the visible. The Unknowable is the Creativeness within that creates, but will ever remain the Uncreated, the Unknowable. The creation can be known, but the Creativeness ever remains unknown.

"Those who seek to corner Reality for their own welfare become antagonistic to others; therefore, there is no love, no expression of the Real, only the self. It is the self that stands in the way."

"Yes, 'I of mine own self am nothing,'" I quoted. "Then Love, Wholeness, comes into Being. In Luke 12:20, I have read these words: 'Thou fool, this night thy soul shall be required of thee; then, whose shall then these things be which thou has provided?" I can see now why prayers, year after year, cannot take the false out of the world. If the teachings of the Masters had not been mutilated to suit the dogmatists and separatists man would have freed himself long ago from imitation, beliefs and ideas, which are causing so much strife in the world."

"I can see also," I continued, "that good prayer is our Love and affection for others; false prayers are words."

"Yes, my son," he said, "it is not an intellectual reaction that is needed, but an expression of Love and affection. So, transformation can take place immediately. Love and affection is action; the intellect merely reacts. Time will not bring It, only an understanding of the self; then there will be an immediate response where memories of right and wrong have passed into oblivion."

As I looked at him I saw that he was enveloped in a light as bright as the sun, and to me came these words, "I am not of this world."

But I knew now that to try to escape from the world could not end its trouble. To isolate myself from the world would be of no value, but what would be of value was to work in it with others, knowing them to be my brothers and sisters, and that what I had was in common with everyone, because all were struggling for freedom but did not know the way to do it.

I saw how all were caught up in a civilisation which we had created overselves with its clash of arms and din of social problems. The world was the people, the people was the world, a world wracked with fear, insecurity and distrust, because they had failed to see the false, thereby failing to understand the true principles of Life which were Love, affection, compassion, forgiveness and good-will.

The world has disregarded the things that mattered while being steeped in the things that did not matter.

Even now we are trying to remedy the effects instead of eliminating the causes. We may well ask ourselves---where are we heading? Not until we embrace the true Christ Principle of living scientifically, individually and collectively, will we be able to look upon the face of the holy man and say "brother."

"I wish I could come with you into your world, my son, but the people would not understand me yet, we will be with you always, even unto the end of the world, for there is no separation between us: the Spiritual and the physical are one. When this is understood the world would emerge from the darkness into the Light that is eternally shining to show mankind the way."

"I am the Light of the world and he who heedeth me shall never know the darkness."

These words passed through my mind as he spoke.

There was a silence for some time; none of us spoke. We were in silent prayer in a way that few would understand.

Then the Hermit spoke. He said: "My son, to-morrow you will be leaving me. In one way I am sorry to see you go, but in another way I am glad. And I am more than glad you came. There is no need to say that I love you as my son."

I felt tears coming into my eyes, and I said: "And I love you as a father, beyond earthly affection."

I had to pull myself together to check the flow of tears. Few can know that true comradeship that comes from the highest motives and true Spiritual understanding. To be with the Hermit was to learn to love all things great and small, for he was the expression of Love itself.

Next morning we were up before day-break, as we had to get over the pass before nightfall. The Hermit came with us part of the way. Several times I looked back at that wonderful sight, the lake, the island, the house and all that it meant to me. It would be the last time I would look upon this scene with my physical eyes, I knew that. So we climbed, one following the other, the Hermit first, then my friend and I came last.

We left the Hermit just above the woodline. We could see him standing there looking towards us as we climbed farther and farther. His long white beard and white hair were blowing in the wind. We climbed and climbed and still the Hermit was there. I said to my friend: "Although there is parting in the physical, thank God there is none in the Spiritual."

"So say I," he echoed.

I stood for a time and waved back to the Hermit, for we would soon be moving out of sight around the rock face to escape the hurricane over the pass and then he would disappear from view.

I said aloud: "I will never again look upon you with my physical eyes. It is a sad moment I feel now."

Then turning to my friend: "There is no separation in the Spiritual. I will leave you also one day, and that will be an even deeper sorrow, but I am glad I came and that we have met in the flesh. And I will rejoice in the knowledge that we are not separated in the Spiritual."

The Hermit had now passed from view. I wondered what he was thinking at that moment.

We climbed now in Indian fashion, there being no room for two on the path. We each had our own thoughts. And they were much the same. We reached the outside of the pass when it was getting dark and we found a cave to shelter in for the night.

We had taken some food with us and we ate it with relish. We wrapped our robes around us and soon fell asleep in the cave that sheltered us from the storm that was howling outside.

Next morning we made our way down to the Tsang Po River to find the man with the coracle waiting for us. My friend spoke to him in Tibetan and said: "But how did you know we were coming?"

He said: "The Hermit came last night and told me you would be here to-day."

When my friend told me this I said: "Wonders will never cease."

We crossed the river and remained at Padong that night. Next morning we started on our long journey of 150 miles to Zamsar. It was a long journey but I loved every bit of it, for my friend---who was more than a friend to me---was a true Spiritual companion whose knowledge was even more astounding than I had first thought. He was a true adept.

The journey and what happened on the way, and what I learned on that never-to-be-forgotten sojourn at Zamsar, will have to be told in another book which I hope to write in the near future.

* * * * * * * *

This present book has been written mainly for enlightenment---not that you will find Truth in any book. It is to be found only within yourself and by yourself; no one else can give It to you.

Chapter XII

Some people think they will understand Life by following experts, by joining philosophical societies or religious organisations. But to know Truth---Reality---there must be freedom from all these things. Freedom can never come through another. It is only when the conditioning influences of belief and the process of accumulated memory are understood that there then comes a silence that is not enforced, and in that silence is the discovery of the Real.

But if your mind is disturbed you are reacting because of your mental formulations, you are caught up in what you believe to be true or not true. With Truth there is no reaction, there is action, and only in Love, Wisdom and Power---And the Kingdom of these---the Kingdom of Heaven---is within you.

Favor

If you enjoyed this book, may I ask a small favor? Please go back to Amazon and leave an honest review of *Beyond the Himalayas*. Reviews help us spread the word of Dr. MacDonald-Bayne to the world more effectively, and sustain our efforts. We appreciate your continued support.

Thank you,
Barry J. Peterson

INTERESTING READS:

"Science and Health, 1875 Edition", Mary Baker Glover (Eddy)
www.ScienceAndHealth1875Edition.Com

"The Sickle" by William W. Walker   www.TheSickle.Org

"The Quimby Manuscripts"   www.TheQuimbyManuscripts.Com

Reading to the Dead, a transitional grief therapy for the living
www.ReadingToTheDead.Com
Author: Barry J Peterson

Neville Goddard: The Complete Reader
www.NevilleGoddardReader.Com
Author: Neville Goddard

www.AudioEnlightenment.Com

GNOSTIC AUDIO SELECTION:
To access the streaming audio book version of
"Beyond the Himalayas"
please visit www.GnosticAudio.Com and follow the directions
to access your free streaming audio version of this publication.
This is streaming audio only; the audio book is NOT downloadable

Visit www.AudioEnlightenmentPress.Com for the latest publications
from the world of Metaphysics

CPSIA information can be obtained
at www.ICGtesting.com
Printed in the USA
BVHW080827050220
571501BV00001B/92